Wood TO Energy

USING SOUTHERN INTERFACE FUELS FOR BIOENERGY

Edited by C. Staudhammer, L.A. Hermansen-Báez, D. Carter, and E.A. Macie

U.S. Department of Agriculture Forest Service
Southern Research Station
General Technical Report GTR-132

The Editors:

Christie Staudhammer, Assistant Professor, Forest Biometrics and **Douglas R. Carter**, Professor, Forest Economics and Management, University of Florida, School of Forest Resources and Conservation, Gainesville, FL 32611; **L. Annie Hermansen-Báez**, Technology Transfer Coordinator, U.S. Department of Agriculture Forest Service, Southern Research Station, Gainesville, FL 32611; **Edward A. Macie**, Regional Urban Forester, U.S. Department of Agriculture Forest Service, Region 8, Atlanta, GA 30309.

Product Disclaimer

The use of trade or firm names in this publication is for reader information and does not imply endorsement by the U.S. Department of Agriculture of any product or service.

January 2011

Southern Research Station
200 W.T. Weaver Blvd.
Asheville, NC 28804

Wood to Energy: Using Southern Interface Fuels for Bioenergy

Edited by:

Christie Staudhammer, L. Annie Hermansen-Báez,
Douglas R. Carter, and Edward A. Macie

Contents

Foreword

Christie Staudhammer

Throughout the United States, a wide variety of efforts are underway to develop economically sound and environmentally sustainable bioenergy production systems. Several Federal policies, such as the Healthy Forests Restoration Act of 2003, support the establishment of biomass-to-energy systems. Scientists in government and nongovernmental agencies are taking the initiative to improve biomass production, processing, and conversion. Entrepreneurs are developing and marketing biobased products for use as bioenergy. Consumers are creating a demand for alternative forms of fuel and power generation. Yet, to advance biomass-based production, there is still a need to educate concerned citizens, community leaders, and those who can supply and use biomass fuels. Potential uses, sources of raw material, and requirements to convert from fossil fuels to biofuels are all topics of concern.

The Southern United States (see **figure** below) produces nearly 60 percent of the Nation's wood, and projections show that this percentage will grow. Many southern forests are located in the wildland-urban interface (WUI), where increased human influence and land use conversion are changing natural resource goods, services, and management (Macie and Hermansen 2002). As populations increase and urban centers spread, large areas of once primarily contiguous forest land are increasingly influenced by humans and surrounded by or intermixed with urban development. The South is a prime location for producing woody biomass for energy production because of the proximity of forests to expanding urban areas, relatively low production costs, and an already abundant wood supply.

The objectives of this document are to increase awareness of potential uses for biomass in WUI areas and to disseminate knowledge about putting bioenergy production systems in place, while addressing issues unique to WUI areas. The South's WUI areas are expanding in population, making them well positioned to take advantage of emerging bioenergy production efforts.

In WUI communities where both the necessary technology and adequate supplies of biomass are available, factors that inhibit immediate implementation of commercial biomass applications include limited awareness and knowledge about putting a biomass energy system in place, as well as a sense of uncertainty about the adequacy of biomass supplies and the costs of biomass sources relative to other energy sources. Potential

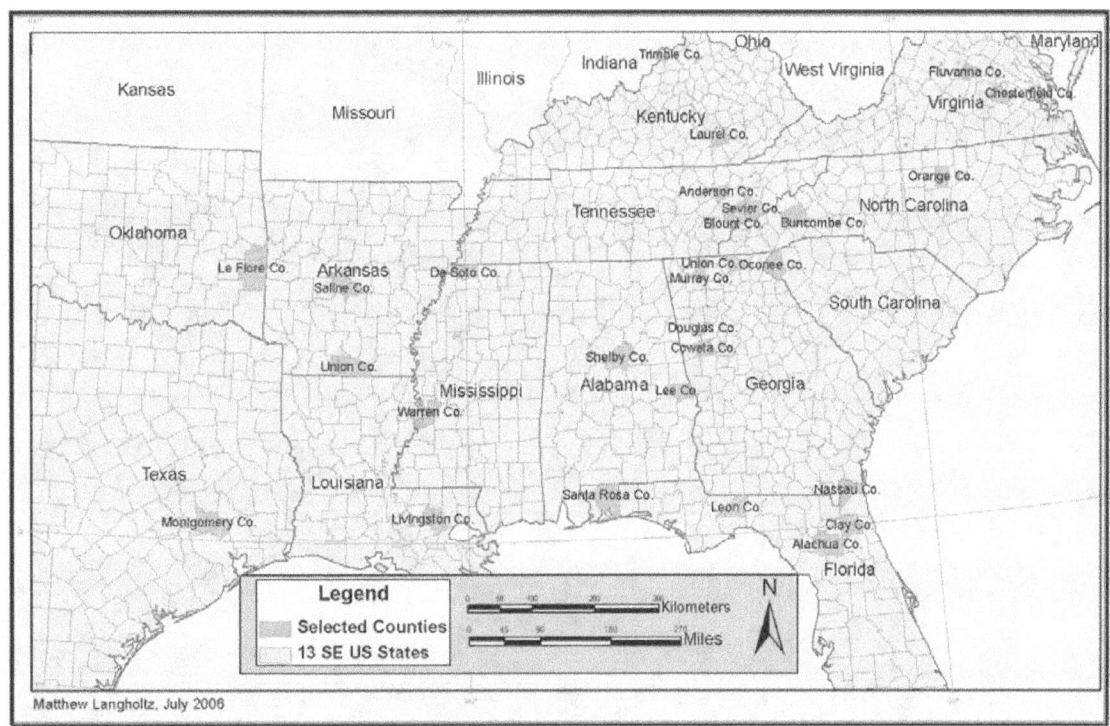

Figure—Map showing the 13 Southern States covered by the Southern Research Station.

woody fuel users—including utility companies, industries, urban tree care industries, local forest landowners, local environmental organizations, and community leaders—need the resources and materials to advocate for implementing biomass fuel systems. This document seeks to remove a key barrier to using woody biomass for energy production by providing information that can help potential wood energy users prepare to bring this novel energy system to their communities.

SCOPE AND SOURCES OF INFORMATION

This report focuses on biomass energy from woody materials in the WUI of the 13 Southern States and Puerto Rico. With a concentration on woody vegetation, we explicitly do not consider other important sources of bioenergy, such as corn-based ethanol and bagasse obtained from sugar cane. The target region of the report differs from other countries and other regions of the United States in many important ways, including climate, vegetation, topography, and demography. The target audience of the report includes resource professionals, the scientific community, and other technical professionals in related fields. Despite the report's specific focus, many of its findings may be applicable to those people who are interested in other sources of bioenergy and who live in other regions.

Information sources for this document include scientific literature, governmental and nongovernmental reports and publications, and interviews with individuals, industry representatives, and citizens and leaders of communities considering bioenergy. More general materials can be found online in the Encyclopedia of Southern Bioenergy (forestencyclopedia.net/Encyclopedia/bioenergy). Because technology advances rapidly, some unpublished data provided by experts in the field is reported and noted accordingly.

Chapter 1
Introduction to Woody Biomass Energy

Christie Staudhammer

Biomass has been defined as the total quantity of organic material in a given area at a particular time. Because biomass is so commonly available, there is a strong tradition of using it for energy in both the United States and abroad. Prior to the industrial revolution, biomass was used to supply almost all human energy needs, and woody biomass in particular was the source of over 90 percent of the total U.S. energy consumption until 1850. In developing countries, biomass is still the dominant source of energy; billions of the world's poor cook and heat with wood and other biomass, accounting for 14 percent of the world's energy use (Sims 2002).

Today, biomass energy is derived from a variety of sources. Europeans take advantage of urban wood waste such as discarded pallets, right-of-way trimmings, and construction debris. In developing nations, rural poor derive biomass energy for heating and cooking from burning animal waste, or from timber cut specifically for this purpose. In the United States, sawmills burn woody residues for power, and some power generating plants have been designed to incorporate agricultural residues such as bagasse, orchard prunings, and nut hulls.

Woody biomass could be an important source of energy in the Southern United States The South represents an important resource for the United States, producing more wood products than any other region of the country (Wear and Greis 2002). In particular, southern wildland-urban interface (WUI) areas, where human development is interspersed with undeveloped wildlands, represent a large forested land base containing a tremendous volume of available biomass. Woody biomass is available as a result of forestry activities such as thinning and harvesting. Increased frequency of natural disasters and conversion of forest land to urban land uses also provides a supply of woody biomass, as does the abundance of waste wood in the WUI. Moreover, potential users are geographically close to sources of biomass, so that the existing infrastructure network can be readily utilized.

BIOENERGY AND WOODY BIOMASS DEFINED

Bioenergy is renewable energy or heat produced from biomass. Biomass includes plant and animal material that can be used as an energy source or for chemical components, e.g., resins, fertilizers, and sugars. Manure, trees, crops, industrial byproducts and effluents, household waste, and forest residues are just a few examples of biomass. Biomass is also recently formed plant material, especially crops grown for their biomass that will be converted to useful energy (Smith 1983). Forest biomass includes accumulated above- and belowground mass, e.g., bark, leaves, and wood, derived from living and dead woody shrubs and trees. In this document, woody biomass includes tree boles, branches, tops, shrubs, hedges, twigs, and residues of wood processing.

Worldwide, wood is the largest source of biomass for energy (National Atlas 2008), and it is the focus of this report. Because the South contains a large portion of readily available woody biomass, forests of the South could be a significant source of woody biomass for energy generation. The varied sources of woody biomass readily available in the WUI areas of the Southern United States are detailed in chapter 2. This includes forest residues from commercial harvests, nonmerchantable biomass from silvicultural activities, and urban wood waste; as well as woody biomass from land restoration and conversion and from short-rotation intensively managed forests.

Use of tops and branches from the merchantable harvest, nonmerchantable timber trees, and understory vegetation helps reduce fire hazard, increase stand productivity, and cut the cost of site preparation. After tree harvesting, woody biomass is commonly chopped, chipped, or pelletized in a preprocessing step and transported to conversion and power generation facilities. It is then converted into fuel, heat, or energy via thermochemical or biochemical processes, such as gasification, biogasification, or pyrolysis. Bioenergy is then produced through a variety of technologies, including steam or gas turbine cycles. Some conversion and power production technologies are more suitable for bioenergy from wood because of the fiber length, moisture content, and other physical and chemical properties of woody biomass. The harvesting and preprocessing of woody biomass for energy and fuels is covered in chapter 3 of this report, while chapter 4 discusses converting woody biomass to heat and energy.

IMPORTANCE OF WOODY BIOMASS AS ENERGY

Worldwide, wood fuels account for 60 percent of total forest product consumption (Food and Agriculture Organization of the United Nations 2008); and in the United States, wood is a significant source of energy. This is especially true of the forest industry, which generates 56 percent of its own energy (American Forest and Paper Association 1996).

While some wood is used in residential heating, most wood is used in larger scale power generation. Even in the most advanced mills, < 50 percent of a tree's wood is made into lumber (Spelter and Alderman 2005). Thus, waste wood products, in the form of sawdust and wood chips, are a major byproduct of industrial sawmill operations, and often are burned to generate power in the wood products industry.

HISTORY OF ENERGY FROM BIOMASS FUELS

The self-sufficiency of the U.S. pulp and paper industries was initiated in the 1970s by energy crises that caused the industry's internal energy production to increase dramatically; between 1972 and 1986, the industry's internal energy production rate nearly doubled to 57 percent (Zerbe 1988).

Worldwide, there is a strong tradition of using biomass fuels in the same geographical region where the fuels are produced (Parikka 2004). Because the Southern United States is a leading producer of forest products, residents of the region have been well positioned to take advantage of local biomass supplies. Beyond the forest products industry, small- and medium-scale bioenergy plants have been built to use these supplies and help other industries mitigate higher energy costs. The Russell Corporation, a textile company in Alabama and Georgia, was the first contemporary nonforest products company to install wood-fired boilers (Zerbe 1988). The Jack Daniel Distillery in Lynchburg, TN, installed two wood-coal-oil-gas-fired boiler systems designed to use primarily green wood wastes from area sawmills and lumber yards.

On a smaller scale, many homes, schools, and small institutions throughout the country use wood wastes to produce < 1 megawatt (MW) for space heating. A medium-sized educational institution in Mississippi uses wood to produce 10 MW of space heat; and schools and hospitals in Vermont, Montana, and Wisconsin use other small-scale bioenergy systems (LeVan-Green 2005).

Across the country, agricultural and forest products residues are used in hundreds of heat and power plants, for a total of almost 10 gigawatt (GW) of installed capacity (Sims 2003 1042 /id). These residues are in the form of branches, broken trees, leaves and needles discarded during harvest (forest residues), as well as sawdust, end cuts, and bark pieces generated during processing (primary process residues). According to Cook and Beyea (2000), about 1.7 exajoule (EJ) of energy are generated annually in the South, from biomass that includes nonwoody sources, but is primarily in fuelwood and residues from the forest products industries.

Bioenergy development in the South and elsewhere, however, has not met its full potential. This shortfall led to the formation of bioenergy roundtables that brought together a range of stakeholders, including farmers, utility companies, and government agencies, with the goal of sharing concerns and engaging in fact finding, negotiating, and consensus building.

The Southeast Bioenergy Roundtable has formulated two strategies: one is to focus on the use of biomass residues and the sustainable development of biomass crop potential to minimize environmental costs and maximize environmental benefits, and the other is to promote bioenergy market development (Cook and Beyea 2000).

In a joint report, the U.S. Department of Energy and the U.S. Department of Agriculture reported that more than 1 billion dry tons of biomass is available each year for energy generation in the United States. This amount could replace 30 percent of U.S. petroleum consumption by 2030, a goal envisioned by the Biomass Research and Development Technical Advisory Committee (the committee was established by the Biomass Research and Development Act of 2000). Of the 1 billion dry tons available each year, 368 million dry tons come from nonmerchantable forest biomass resources. Depending on timber markets and energy prices, an additional 7.9 million dry tons are potentially available from commercial forest thinnings in the South (Perlack and others 2005). Chapter 5 of this report examines the supply of woody biomass in the WUI of the Southern United States, and chapter 6 presents an economic analysis of this supply.

TRENDS IN POPULATION AND ENERGY USE IN THE SOUTH

Between 1990 and 2000, the population of the United States increased 13 percent, while the South's population increased 18 percent (U.S. Census Bureau 2000). The South now accounts for 34 percent of the total U.S. population. By 2020, the South's population is expected to increase another 26 percent (Cordell and Macie 2002). This trend is driven by migration from other U.S. regions and from abroad. Over the period 1990 to 2000, net migration to the Southern United States was greater than to all other U.S. regions combined (U.S. Census Bureau 2000).

As the population of the United States has grown, so has the country's energy consumption. From 1985 to 2005, energy consumption in the United States grew by an average of 2 percent per year; moreover, while the United States accounts for < 5 percent of the world's population, it consumes about 22 percent of the world's energy (Energy Information Administration 2008).

From 1994 to 2004, per capita energy consumption in the United States increased from 215 to 340 million British thermal units (Energy Information Administration 2005). In the Southeast in particular, electricity demand represents a relatively larger share of total U.S. electricity sales, and the Southeast's need for new electricity capacity is greater than in other regions of the country (Energy Information Administration 2006). Residential-delivered energy use is projected to increase by 9 percent between 2003 and 2010, up 23 percent by 2025, with 68 percent of this growth expected to come from increased use of electricity. Projected housing growth in the South, where almost all new homes will use central air conditioning, is an important component of the projection, as is increased use of consumer electronics across the country (Energy Information Administration 2005). In the southern WUI, bioenergy can help meet this projected increase in demand for energy.

TRENDS IN LAND USE CHANGE IN THE WILDLAND-URBAN INTERFACE

The median age of residents in the South and elsewhere is rising, and by 2020, more than 17 percent of people in the region will be over 65. While the population growth is occurring mostly in urban areas, driving new development and expansion of the WUI, rural areas are also expected to grow by 12 percent (Cordell and Macie 2002).

Meanwhile, the trend in the 1990s toward large-scale conversion from rural to urban development indicates that new rural residents can contribute substantially to the expansion of WUI areas. Most of the rural South's private landowners maintain a strong conservation ethic, but as these landowners get older, they are selling their land, a recent trend that makes predictions from historical patterns difficult. Nevertheless, population growth is expected in many counties that are heavily forested, which will create pressure for development as well as timber harvesting. Additionally, as urbanization and population expands into rural areas, there will be additional pressures on lands for recreation and wildlife habitat. In interface communities, jobs in forestry, mining, and fisheries have been stable and are projected to remain so (Cordell and Macie 2002). However, farming has employed ever smaller proportions of the South's workforce, a trend that is expected to continue its decline. Jobs are projected to shift from farming and manufacturing to service, retail, technology, and other urban industries, a change that will result in higher wages on average. In turn, higher average wages likely will cause further housing development in the WUI and increased energy demands.

STRATEGIES IN U.S. ENERGY POLICY

Over the last decade, proposed energy strategies for the United States have included increasing energy efficiency, storing carbon in forests and other ecosystems, and displacing fossil fuels with energy sources that are CO_2 neutral (Cook and Beyea 2000). CO_2-neutral energy sources are balanced with respect to how much carbon is produced in their making versus how much carbon is released in their use, i.e., no net carbon emissions result from CO_2-neutral energy sources.

In recognition of the potential socioeconomic and environmental benefits from bioenergy generation, the Farm Bill 2002, Title IX, provides loan guarantees and grants to farmers, ranchers, and small business owners who support renewable energy projects in rural areas. Other sections of Title IX provide for Federal procurement of biobased products, biomass research and development, and continuation of the bioenergy program. Similarly, the Energy Policy Act of 2005 provides for grants, credits, loan guarantees, incentive payments, and Federal mandates relevant to the production of biopower and biofuels, including grants to improve commercialization of forest biomass for electricity generation and other energy conversion processes. The Policy Act also amends the Biomass Research and Development Act of 2000 by adding provisions for regional bioeconomy development grants.

Climate change legislation supports bioenergy development, with the Sense of the Senate on Climate Change Resolution (passed June 22, 2005) bringing greater attention to environmental problems that bioenergy can mitigate (Smith 2005). The 2007 Farm Bill confirmed this support, improving and increasing funding for the bioenergy program and creating a biomass energy reserve program to develop new feedstocks for renewable energies, such as cellulosic ethanol. Moreover, Title VIII of the bill established a Forest Bioenergy Research Program, providing $75 million to address issues related to woody biomass for bioenergy production (U.S. House of Representatives 2008).

While increased energy efficiency is a long-term strategy, there is also public pressure to address other ecological and social challenges, including air quality in urban and rural areas, ecological integrity and biodiversity on cropland and forests, trade deficit and national security costs of petroleum, and markets for wood waste and less desirable wood (Cook and Beyea 2000). Chapter 7 discusses public perceptions of biomass and new interest in bioenergy as it pertains to community environmental and economic sustainability.

SOCIAL, ECONOMIC, AND ENVIRONMENTAL BENEFITS OF BIOENERGY

Potential social, economic, and environmental benefits of bioenergy are widely recognized. The major environmental benefit of bioenergy is the reduction of greenhouse gas emissions. When fossil fuels are displaced by sustainably produced biomass fuels, CO_2 released in power generation is mitigated by carbon resequestered from the atmosphere as biomass stocks regrow. Greenhouse gas emissions are also reduced by increasing the amount of carbon stored onsite, e.g., by reforestation of agricultural lands or mined lands. During photosynthesis, trees absorb CO_2 and break it down into oxygen and carbon. Oxygen is released back into the atmosphere, and the carbon is stored (sequestered) in the tree stem, branches, and roots. Thus, if treeless landscapes are replaced by forested land, there will be a net carbon accumulation on these sites. Reforestation and afforestation can also create other environmental benefits, including better soil and water quality, as well as improved wildlife habitat that consists of greater biological and structural diversity.

Localized environmental problems, such as nitrogen oxide (NO_x), sulfur oxide (SO_x), and mercury emissions, can also be mitigated through reduced fossil fuel combustion, because bioenergy production systems release far lower levels of these compounds into the atmosphere (Marland and others 2000; Sims 2002, 2003). Creating markets for woody biomass can offset costs of thinning overgrown or diseased forest stands, measures that can improve forest health and reduce forest fuel loads and fire risk in the WUI. Planting and maintaining forests can also help control encroachment of fire-intolerant or invasive trees, restore native ecosystems, and make forested land more economically competitive through alternative land uses, all of which maintains green space in developing areas.

Short-rotation woody crops (SRWC) used as dedicated energy fuel supply systems can reduce nutrient loading from reclaimed waste water and other urban and rural wastes, restore mined lands, and control invasive exotics such as cogongrass *(Imperata cylindrica)* (Rockwood and others 2004). Furthermore, SRWC systems typically sequester more carbon, require less fertilization and energy inputs, cause less soil erosion, and have higher biodiversity values than conventional agricultural systems (Tobert and Wright 1998, Tobert and others 2000). Socioeconomic benefits from bioenergy include not only energy security through reduced dependence on imported oil but also generation of employment and resulting economic multiplier effects in rural communities.

POTENTIAL NEGATIVE CONSEQUENCES OF BIOMASS ENERGY PRODUCTION IN THE WILDLAND-URBAN INTERFACE

Potential negative consequences from biomass energy production in the WUI include losses of natural areas, e.g., temporary loss from harvest and planting of SRWC, air pollution, soil nutrient depletion, and potentially higher costs for energy. The impacts of biomass energy production on the environment are comparable to those of conventional forestry practices in WUI areas, and less than those associated with agricultural land uses; moreover, appropriate management practices can mitigate the impacts.

Obtaining woody biomass from waste sources of wood is inexpensive and does not affect standing plantations and natural areas. However, using wood obtained from conventional logging practices has a direct impact on the forest environment, such as wildlife habitat loss and soil compaction, and some biomass generating activities, e.g., precommercial thinning, may be expensive (Koning and Skog 1987). As harvesting specifically for woody biomass becomes more commonplace, advances in technology likely will mitigate costs (Zerbe 1988). In some parts of the United States and elsewhere, overthinning young, high quality trees could lead to a loss of future high value timber (Koning and Skog 1987). However, in the South, due to a large number of overstocked stands, thinning is a common and beneficial silvicultural treatment that promotes higher quality timber growth and guards against southern pine beetle outbreaks (Florida Department of Agriculture & Consumer Services 2008).

A more substantive concern is that removal of thinned material might result in the loss of valuable nutrients in the woody

materials that are removed from the site (Parikka 2004). However, fertilization and other silvicultural practices can alleviate the loss.

Another concern is that biomass energy production might result in the conversion of natural areas to plantations, leading to reduced biodiversity from an impaired ecosystem function (Cook and Beyea 2000), or increased disturbance from higher impact or reentry logging practices (Fung and others 2002). Silvicultural practices favor faster growing species or lead to increased fertilizer and pesticide use could reduce biodiversity (Fung and others 2002) and negatively impact wildlife and recreation (Koning and Skog 1987). Some researchers, e.g., Patzek and Pimentel 2005, have warned of potential degradation of soil nutrients, structure, and diversity in industrial biomass production. These concerns, however, are comparable to those of conventional forestry. Moreover, if land conversion takes place in agricultural areas in the WUI, these pressures will be mitigated by promoting land use more consistent with historical natural patterns.

Air pollution concerns arise from the harvest, transportation, and energy conversion of woody biomass. Indirect emissions come from energy carriers during transportation and extraction (Wahlund and Westermark 2004). During combustion, particulate-derived pollution produced with wood can be high because of the still prevalent use of obsolete conversion technologies, e.g., residential homes with conventional wood-burning fireplaces, and because of poorly developed emissions controls (Zerbe 1988). Furthermore, wood waste from building sites and demolition may contain preservative treated and painted wood, which could result in the release of toxic residues if materials are not sorted prior to combustion.

The biggest barrier to biomass energy adoption is not technical but rather economic (Hoffmann and Weih 2005). High costs are associated with harvesting, collecting, and especially transporting biomass fuels (Wahlund and Westermark 2004, Zerbe 1988). Moreover, there is a lack of infrastructure for marketing biomass fuel products, and with some notable exceptions in some geographic areas, there is no viable market for young, thinned material. Market development will not take place until biomass suppliers have a guarantee that they will have buyers over the long term, and utility companies will not invest in biomass conversion technologies unless they have a guaranteed economically viable supply of biomass. The impasse means that both the utility industry and forest products industry are reluctant to make capital investments without long-term contracts (Zerbe 1988). Utilizing fuel wood from the WUI and locating conversion and power facilities nearby, however, will mitigate most of these costs, and forested WUI communities that have leaders knowledgeable about their woody biomass supply are well poised to make appropriate long-term commitments.

A further change in energy policy could help make these capital investments occur. The U.S. Government continues to subsidize coal, oil, natural gas, and nuclear power. Federal subsidies for primary energy in year 2007 were estimated at $11.2 billion (Energy Information Administration 2007). Other countries, including Sweden and Norway, have introduced carbon tax policies that partly level the playing field among energy technologies (Fischer and Newell 2004, Hoffmann and Weih 2005). Sweden has made biomass attractive through government subsidies for short-rotation plantations, higher taxes on fossil fuels, and the creation of a biofuel market.

CONCLUSIONS

Woody biomass is a viable alternative to conventional fossil fuels, and fits well with proposed U.S. energy strategies to promote carbon-neutral energy sources. As the South's population and energy demands increase, the region is well-positioned to take advantage of woody biomass sources. The South is home to a large and long-established forest products industry that produces an abundant supply of woody biomass materials, especially true in expanding interface areas subject to land conversion pressures.

Careful planning can mitigate most negative consequences of obtaining and using woody biomass. Some issues, such as high transportation costs, are substantially of less concern in the WUI where bioenergy plants and woody biomass sources are often close geographically. Moreover, where forestry practices replace traditional agriculture, most negative consequences all but disappear. The positive externalities associated with woody biomass include benefits to the soil, water, atmosphere, environment, and community. Forests filter impurities, providing clean water, and continuous forest cover helps control erosion. Using woody biomass will have positive environmental impacts through reduced NO_x and SO_x emissions and increased carbon sequestration. Moreover, afforestation and reforestation will promote habitat restoration and biodiversity. Finally, bioenergy projects using woody biomass will create positive local and regional economic impacts for WUI communities and rural areas. Using woody biomass as an alternative energy source can help preserve natural areas and reduce reliance on fossil fuels.

REFERENCES

Anon. 2005. Forest management: introduction to the southern pine beetle (SPB). http://www.fl-dof.com/forest_management/fh_insects_spb.html. 4 p. [Date accessed: January 8, 2010].

American Forest and Paper Association. 1996. Fact sheet on 1994 energy use in the U.S. pulp and paper industry. Washington, DC. 1 p.

Bergman, R.; Zerbe, J.I. 2004. Primer on wood biomass for energy. http://www.fpl.fs.fed.us/documnts/tmu/biomass_energy/primer_on_wood_biomass_for_energy.pdf, 10 p. [Date accessed: January 8, 2010].

Cook, J.; Beyea, J. 2000. Bioenergy in the United States: progress and possibilities. Biomass and Bioenergy. 18: 441–455.

Cordell, H.K.; Macie, E.A. 2002. Population and demographic trends. In: Macie, E.A.; Hermansen, L.A., eds. Human influences on forest ecosystems: the southern wildland-urban interface assessment. Gen. Tech. Rep. SRS–55. Asheville, NC: U.S. Department of Agriculture Forest Service, Southern Research Station: 11–34.

Drew, A.P.; Zsuffa, L.; Mitchell, C.P. 1987. Terminology relating to woody plant biomass and its production. Biomass. 12: 79–82.

Energy Information Administration. 1999. Federal financial interventions and subsidies in energy markets 1999: primary energy. SR/OIAF/99–03. Washington, DC. 132 p.

Energy Information Administration. 2005. Annual energy review 2004. U.S. DOE DOE/EIA–0384(2004). Washington, DC. 206 p.

Energy Information Administration. 2006. Annual energy outlook 2006. Washington, DC: U.S. Department of Energy, Office of Integrated Analysis and Forecasting. 236 p.

Energy Information Administration. 2007. Federal financial interventions and subsidies in energy markets 2007. SR/CNEAF/2008–01. Washington, DC. 274 p.

Energy Information Administration. 2008. Official energy statistics from the U.S. Government. http://www.eia.doe.gov/emeu/international/energyconsumption.html. [Date accessed: March 3].

Fischer, C.; Newell, R. 2004. Environmental and technology policies for climate change and renewable energy. Resour. for the Future Discussion Paper 04–05. Washington, DC: Resources for the Future. 47 p.

Florida Department of Agriculture & Consumer Services, Division of Forestry. 2008. Forest management: introduction to the southern pine beetle (SPB). http://www.fl-dof.com/forest_management/fh_insects_spb.html. [Date accessed: March 3].

Food and Agriculture Organization of the United Nations. 2008. FAO forestry facts and figures. http://www.fao.org/forestry/site/28679/en/. [Date accessed: March 3].

Fung, P.Y.H.; Kirschbaum, M.U.F.; Raison, R.J.; Stucley, C. 2002. The potential for bioenergy production from Australian forests, its contribution to national greenhouse targets and recent developments in conversion processes. Biomass and Bioenergy. 22: 223–236.

Hermansen, L.A.; Macie, E.A. 2002. Introduction. In: Macie, E.A.; Hermansen, L.A., eds. Human influences on forest ecosystems: the southern wildland-urban interface assessment. Gen. Tech. Rep. SRS–55. Asheville, NC: U.S. Department of Agriculture Forest Service, Southern Research Station: 1–10.

Hoffmann, D.; Weih, M. 2005. Limitations and improvement of the potential utilisation of woody biomass for energy derived from short rotation woody crops in Sweden and Germany. Biomass and Bioenergy. 28: 267–279.

Koning, J.W.; Skog, K.E. 1987. Use of wood energy in the United States - an opportunity. Biomass. 12: 27–36.

LeVan-Green, S. 2005. Commercialization, potential uses, and application of bioenergy in the South. http://biomass.sref.info/proceedings.htm. In: Status, Trends, and Future of the South's Forest and Agricultural Biomass Conference Proceedings. [Date accessed: January 8, 2010].

Macie, E.A.; Hermansen, L.A., eds. 2002. Human influences on forest ecosystems: the southern wildland-urban interface assessment. Gen. Tech. Rep. SRS–55. Asheville, NC: U.S. Department of Agriculture Forest Service, Southern Research Station. 162 p.

Marland, G.; Wigley, T.M.L.; Schimel, D.S. 2000. The future role of reforestation in reducing buildup of atmospheric CO_2. In: The carbon cycle. Cambridge, MA: Cambridge University Press. 292 p.

National Atlas. 2008. Renewable energy sources in the United States. http://www.nationalatlas.gov/articles/people/a_energy.html, [Date accessed: March 3].

Parikka, M. 2004. Global biomass fuel resources. Biomass and Bioenergy. 27: 613–620.

Patzek, T.W.; Pimental, D. 2005. Thermodynamics of energy production from biomass. Critical Reviews in Plant Science. 24(5–6): 327–364.

Perlack, R.; Wright, L.; Turhollow, A.F. [and others]. 2005. Biomass as feedstock for a bioenergy and bioproducts industry: the technical feasibility of a billion-ton annual supply. ORNL/TM–2005/66. Washington, DC: U.S. Department of Energy; U.S. Department of Agriculture Forest Service. 73 p.

Rockwood, D.L.; Naidu, C.; Segrest, S. [and others]. 2004. Short-rotation woody crops and phytoremediation: opportunities for agroforestry? In: New vistas in agroforestry, a compendium for the 1st World Congress of agroforestry 2004. Dordrecht, The Netherlands: Kluwer Academic Publishers: 51–63.

Sims, R. 2003. Bioenergy options for a cleaner environment in developed and developing countries. Amsterdam, The Netherlands: Elsevier. 198 p.

Sims, R.E.H. 2002. The brilliance of bioenergy in business and in practice. London: James & James Ltd. 316 p.

Smith, S. 2005. Future of bioenergy: national overview of energy initiatives for agriculture and forestry. In: Status, Trends, and Future of the South's Forest and Agricultural Biomass Conference Proceedings. [Date accessed: January 8, 2010].

Smith, W.H. 1983. Energy from biomass: a new commodity. In: Rosenblum, J.W., ed. Agriculture in the twenty-first century. New York: Wiley & Sons: 61-69.

Spelter, H.; Alderman, M. 2005. Profile 2005: softwood sawmills in the United. States and Canada. Res. Pap. FPL–RP–630. Madison, WI: U.S. Department of Agriculture Forest Service, Forest Products Laboratory. 85 p.

Tolbert, V.R.; Thornton, F.C.; Joslin, J.D. [and others]. 2000. Increasing belowground carbon sequestration with conversion of agricultural lands to production of bio-energy crops. New Zealand Journal of Forestry Science. 30(1–2): 138–149.

Tolbert, V.R.; Wright, L.L. 1998. Environmental enhancement of U.S. biomass crop technologies: research results to date. Biomass and Bioenergy. 15(1): 93–100.

U.S. Census Bureau. 2000. U.S. census 2000 resident population. http://www.census.gov/population/www/cen2000/maps/respop.html. [Date accessed: March 17, 2007].

U.S. House of Representatives, House Committee on Agriculture. 2008. 2007 Farm Bill forestry title. http://www.agriculture.house.gov/inside/Legislation/110/FB/Forestry%20Title.pdf. [Date accessed: March 3].

Wahlund, B.; Yan, J.; Westermark, M. 2004. Increasing biomass utilization in energy systems: a comparative study of CO_2 reduction and cost for different bioenergy processing options. Biomass and Bioenergy. 26: 531–544.

Wear, David N.; Greis, John G., eds. 2002. Southern forest resource assessment. Gen. Tech. Rep. SRS–53. Asheville, NC: U.S. Department of Agriculture Forest Service, Southern Research Station. 635 p.

Zerbe, J.I. 1988. Biofuels: production and potential. Forum for Applied Research and Public Policy. Winter: 38–47.

Glossary of Terms

bioenergy: heat and/or electricity produced from biomass energy systems, usually measured in J (J of energy per gram of fuel), MJ/g, or GJ/g.

biofuels: liquid fuels made from biomass, which are used for transportation or cooling.

biogas: a gas that is produced from biomass that is usually combustible.

biomass: plant and animal material that can be used as an energy source or for chemical components; e.g., trees, crops, algae and other plants, agricultural and forest residues, organic industrial byproducts and household waste, food manufacturing effluents, sludges, and manures.

Btu: British thermal unit. A standard unit of energy that is the amount of energy equal to the heat required to increase the temperature of 1 pound of water 1 degree Fahrenheit.

cofiring: introducing biomass as a supplemental energy source in coal plants.

cogeneration: the simultaneous production of heat and electricity from a single fuel, also called combined heat and power.

comminution: reduction of woody biomass to wood chips, e.g., by hammermill or chipper.

forest biomass: the accumulated above- and belowground mass, including bark, leaves, and wood, from living and dead woody shrubs and trees.

forest residues: the aboveground materials generated from logging during precommercial thinnings and harvesting operations, e.g., leaves, bark, tops, and broken trees.

fuel preprocessing: techniques for producing upgraded biomass fuel, such as drying and densification, which can lead to more homogenous, higher energy content fuels.

gross primary production: total amount of organic matter produced as trees convert carbon dioxide and water to solar energy through photosynthesis.

hog fuel: biomass generated by grinding wood and wood waste for use in a combustor.

industrial forestry process residues: residues that result from the incomplete use of wood raw material.

joule (J): a unit of electrical energy; 1 MJ is the amount of energy needed to raise a 1 mt object to a height of 100 m. (On average, 54,000 MJ of energy are needed to heat a single family house for 1 year under continental climate conditions.)

kilowatt: rate of electrical power output.

logging residues: poor quality trees and tree components, such as crowns and stump-root systems that are left onsite during commercial harvesting operations.

net biomass increment: change in accumulated biomass over a measurement period.

net primary production: the photosynthates that are not consumed during respiration, but are incorporated into the various tree components during the assimilation process.

precommercial thinning: a silvicultural treatment or type of cut in which young trees are removed to promote growth of the remaining trees.

primary process residues: residues that result from primary wood processing, e.g., lumber, veneer, pulp, and paper, such as bark, sawdust, cores, slabs, and black liquor.

pyrolysis: the process of combusting during oxygen-starved conditions, which involves the physical and chemical decomposition of solid organic matter by heating into liquid, gas, and carbon char residue.

secondary process residues: residues that result from secondary wood processing, e.g., furniture manufacturing, such as sawdust and small scrap wood.

short-rotation crops: crops, such as rapeseed, grown and harvested for biomass production over a short time frame.

short-rotation forests: trees, such as eucalypts, grown and harvested for biomass production over a short time frame, usually 5 years or less.

short-rotation woody crops (SRWC): a silvicultural system based upon short clear-felling cycles, generally between 1 and 15 years, employing intensive cultural techniques such as fertilization, irrigation and weed control, and utilizing genetically superior planting material (Drew and Mitchell 1987).

silvicultural residues: trees smaller than merchantable size that are left intact at the site of precommercial thinnings.

wildland-urban interface (WUI): areas where increased human influence and land use conversion are changing natural resource goods, services, and management (Hermansen and Macie 2002).

wood residues: the waste materials generated from wood processing operations, e.g., bark, wood chips, sawdust, and broken lumber.

Chapter 2

Woody Biomass Sources in the Wildland-Urban Interface

Christie Staudhammer, Richard Schroeder, Brian Becker, and Matthew Langholtz

INTRODUCTION

The wildland-urban interface (WUI) in the Southern United States contains a variety of woody biomass sources that could be used for bioenergy. The WUI is defined as the area where human development is interspersed with undeveloped wildlands. In the South, these wildlands are fragmented by commercial and residential development and composed primarily of private forest lands.

Southern forest lands represent an important resource for the United States, producing more wood products than any other region in the Nation (Wear and Greis 2002). The nature and trends of land ownership and use in the South influence the availability of woody biomass. Conversion of agricultural land to forest land has increased the annual yield of forest products, while clearing of forested lands for urban use has produced one-time harvests of available woody biomass. Concurrently, a slowing pulpwood market has depressed stumpage prices for small-diameter trees, leaving many forests overstocked due to the increased cost of thinning and increasing the availability of low-cost woody biomass.

Woody biomass users in the South can also benefit from having various sources of residue, including timber harvests, thinnings of plantations and natural stands, urban wood residue from yard trimmings, commercial tree care industry and utility line clearings, municipal solid waste, invasive plant removal, native plant restoration, and phytoremediation projects. Because the South contains a large portion of readily available woody biomass, the working forests of the South could be a significant source of woody biomass for energy generation. This chapter reviews the varieties of woody biomass that can be found in the WUI of the South.

FOREST RESOURCES IN THE WILDLAND-URBAN INTERFACE

Forest resources in the WUI consist of three primary components: (1) merchantable standing timber, (2) forest residues from commercial harvests, and (3) nonmerchantable timber removals. Since merchantable timber has higher value alternative markets, woody biomass resources for energy are likely to be limited to the remaining nonmerchantable components, which include trees that have not attained sufficient size, are of poor quality, or are nonmerchantable species, as well as residue material produced in the course of forestry activities.

These materials, including forest residues as well as the products of precommercial thinnings and fuel mitigation harvests, are the primary source of forest residue biomass (Perlack and others 2005). Forest residues from commercial harvests and nonmerchantable timber removals are often grouped with mill residues such as sawdust and bark to form what is known as "total forest residues." In this context, "nonmerchantable biomass resources" refers to resources that have no conventional timber forest product market, although, if bioenergy markets are developed, nonmerchantable forest and urban residues could have commercial value. However, for the foreseeable future, it is likely that energy wood will be the lowest valued wood product harvested from the forest.

THE SOUTHERN FOREST RESOURCE

The amount of woody biomass available for energy in the Southern United States is strongly linked to the amount of forest land and the level of forest operations undertaken in the region. The Forest Service defines forest land as "land at least 10 percent stocked by forest trees of any size, including land that formerly had such tree cover and that will be naturally or artificially regenerated." Timber lands are defined as "forest land that is producing or is capable of producing crops of industrial wood," while reserved lands are those that have been "withdrawn from timber utilization by statute or administrative regulation" (Smith and others 2004). The South makes up 24 percent of the total area of the United States but 40 percent of U.S. timberland (totaling 203 million acres, or 82 million ha), making the South the largest timberland region in the United States **(fig. 2.1)**. With its large

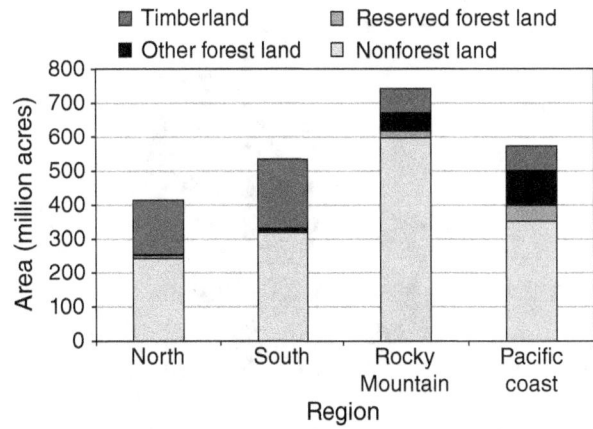

Figure 2.1—Area of major forest land types by U.S. Department of Agriculture Forest Service region (adapted from Smith and others 2004).

Table 2.1—Land area in the South by major class and State, 2002

State	Total land area[a]	Land class				Other land
		Forest land				
		Total forest land[b]	Timberland	Reserved	Other	
		thousand acres				
Alabama	32,481	22,987	22,922	65	0	9,494
Arkansas	33,328	18,771	18,373	231	167	14,557
Florida	34,520	16,285	14,636	1,121	528	18,235
Georgia	37,067	24,404	23,802	595	7	12,663
Kentucky	25,428	12,684	12,347	305	32	12,744
Louisiana	27,883	13,812	13,722	90	0	14,071
Mississippi	30,025	18,580	18,572	8	0	11,445
Oklahoma	43,955	7,665	6,234	45	1,386	36,290
North Carolina	31,180	19,302	18,664	598	40	11,878
South Carolina	19,272	12,495	12,301	194	0	6,777
Tennessee	26,381	14,396	13,956	440	0	11,985
Texas	167,626	17,149	11,774	125	5,250	150,477
Virginia	25,342	16,073	15,371	686	16	9,269
South total	534,488	214,603	202,674	4,503	7,426	319,885

[a] Total land area is comprised of Total forest land and Other land.
[b] Total forest land is comprised of Timberland, Reserved, and Other.
Source: Smith and others (2004).

timberland area and long growing season, the South contributed 63 percent of the U.S. timber harvest in 2001, up from 51 percent in 1986 (Smith and others 2004). Land class details for the South by State are shown in **table 2.1**.

In 2003, 5 million private landowners owned 89 percent of the South's 215 million forest acres. As shown in **figure 2.2**, in 1999, 69 percent (138 million) of the 203 million acres of timberland

in the South was nonindustrial private forest and 20 percent (40 million) was owned by forest industry (Wear and Greis 2002). Plantations were approximately 19 percent (35 million acres) private forests and 8 percent (2 million acres) public forests (Smith and others 2004).

Timberland acreages in the South have been fairly stable since the 1950s, but the South's privately owned forests have been in flux and are influenced by various social and economic factors. For example, gains in forest area from abandoned agricultural lands have been offset by conversion of southern forests to urban development (Wear and Greis 2002). Pine plantations in the South are projected to increase to 54 million acres by 2040, a 60-percent increase from 1995 (Wear and Greis 2002). Pine plantations in southern private forests are projected to increase 14 million acres by 2050, associated with a 15- and 18-percent decline in natural pine and upland hardwood forests, respectively (Alig and others 2002).

Trends in timber prices are indicative of the relative scarcity of forest products and can indicate the strength of the forest industry in the South. Between 1988 and 1998, prices of hardwood pulpwood, softwood pulpwood, and softwood sawtimber increased at rates of 12, 5, and 8 percent, respectively. Hardwood sawtimber prices increased 6 percent between 1992 and 1998, reflecting a scarcity of timber products during that period. However, since 1998, the southern timber markets have been in a period of transition. In 2005, southern softwood pulpwood

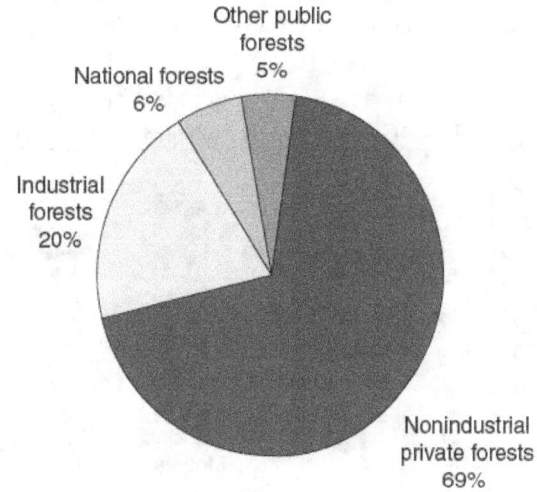

Figure 2.2—Distribution of 203 million acres of Southern U.S. timberland in 1999 (Wear and Greis 2002).

prices fell to their lowest since 1997 (Wear and others 2005); and southern pulpwood production declined from 181 in 1994 to 162 million green tons in 2003 (Johnson and Steppleton 2005). Since 1998, prices for other timber products have leveled or declined.

The market decline has been attributed to a combination of technological change, product substitution, pulpmill capacity decline, increased imports, use of recycled materials, and some loss of competitive advantage to mills in Latin America (Wear and others 2005). In spite of the timber market contraction since 1998, demand for forest products is projected to continue as domestic and international populations increase, and softwood inventories in the South are projected to exceed current growing stock through 2040, with hardwood inventories peaking in 2025 (Adams and others 2003, Wear and Greis 2002). Small-diameter timber currently sold for pulpwood could be an economically viable resource for energy under conditions of low wood prices and high energy costs.

FOREST RESIDUES FROM COMMERCIAL HARVEST

Perlack and others (2005) estimated that 368 million dry tons per year of sustainably available biomass could be obtained from forest lands nationwide, primarily from forest residues, silvicultural treatments, and fuelwood extractions. The amount is more than twice what is currently used for bioenergy from both agriculture and forestry resources. Estimates based on the Timber Product Output (TPO) Database Retrieval System (U.S. Department of Agriculture Forest Service 2005) indicate that 49 million dry tons of logging residue could be obtained annually nationwide. In the South, 17.5 million dry tons of logging residue was produced in 2002. Though not all logging residue can or should be harvested for biofuels, even a small percentage of this total represents a significant resource. Removals and forest residues by hardwood and softwood class for each Southern State are shown in **figure 2.3**.

Forest residues consist of four major components: (1) tops, (2) limbs, (3) stumps, (4) and unutilized cull trees. In a recent study in east Texas, 17.6 percent of the total logging residue was stumps, with the remainder in tops, limbs, and culls (Xu and Carraway 2005). While roots and stumps can be a significant part of plantation biomass, the cost associated with recovery is high, the wood is often contaminated with soil, and ecological studies suggest that removal might not be desirable (Hakkila and Parikka 2002). Tops, branches, and small stems, often referred to as logging slash, present harvesting and handling challenges because this material is generally less than one-fourth the density of solid wood, which increases the harvesting cost per ton (Rummer and others 2004). Moreover, skidding logs from the stump site to the landing tends to leave the tops contaminated with soil and stones. Soil contamination results in high levels of ash when biomass is combusted, leading to slagging and fouling which can cause damage to furnaces and boilers (Sims and Bassam 2003).

In conventional forestry, forest residues not directly utilized are left in the forest to degrade naturally for the recycling of nutrients, discarded in piles or windrowed for wildlife habitat, or burned on site for disposal. Burning in a boiler for bioenergy would reduce the pollution associated with open burning and the release of methane (a greenhouse gas) caused by material decomposition. Forest residues utilized for bioenergy usually go straight from the forest to a chip pile with 40 to 50 percent moisture and are burned "as is." Field drying of forest residues can reduce the moisture content and grinding will increase the density, reducing the haul cost per British thermal unit (Btu), which results in more cost-effective handling. However, allowing material to air-dry in the field for several weeks will increase travel costs, as multiple trips to the harvest site would be required. Estimates of available forest residues can be found in the Forest Service, Southern Forest

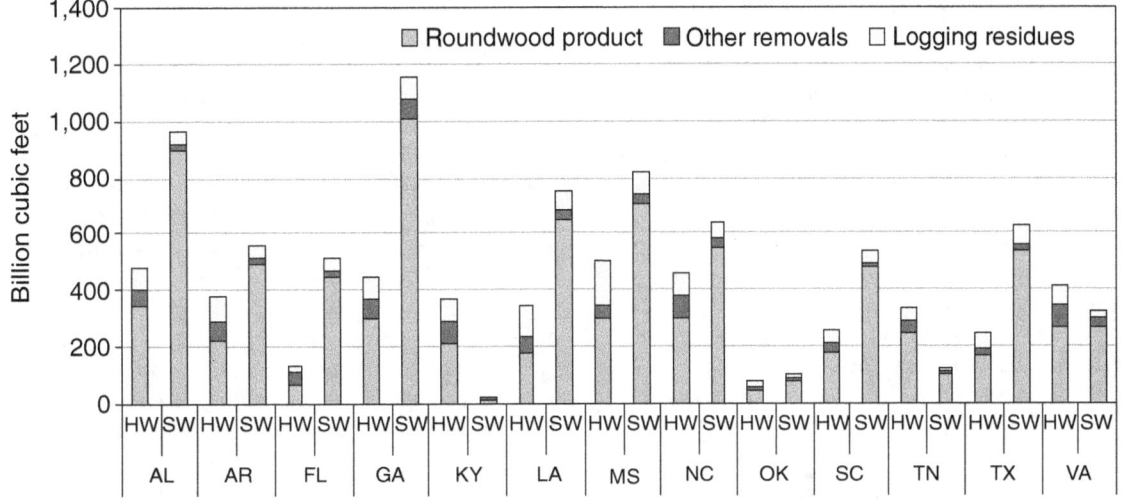

Figure 2.3—Volume (bcf) of roundwood product, other removals, and logging residues for hardwoods (HW) and softwoods (SW), 2002.

Resource Assessment (U.S. Department of Agriculture Forest Service 2004).

NONMERCHANTABLE BIOMASS FROM SILVICULTURAL ACTIVITIES

Most of the nonmerchantable biomass resource in the South is associated with conventional forestry operations, which usually include silvicultural activities, such as precommercial thinning to improve the quality of future harvests, and preventative treatments, such as insect or fuel reduction harvests. In the Southern United States, many silvicultural activities are driven by concerns about overstocked forests (Wolfe 2000), especially in the WUI where traditional forestry activities are often restricted.

Forests with an overabundance of small-diameter trees require thinning because the forests are at increased risk for insect outbreaks, such as the southern pine beetle. Moreover, overstocked forests have a higher risk of fire, and as WUI populations increase, the threat to residential and commercial structures from wildfire in forests within and adjacent to the WUI increases. Public concern over smoke and out-of-control fires raises questions about controlled burning as a fuel-mitigation strategy (Shindler and Toman 2003). This has led some communities to explore fuel mitigation harvesting for bioenergy (Farnsworth and others 2003). Perlack and others (2005) estimated that material from thinnings in the South could produce 8 million dry tons annually, at a low cost.

For either silvicultural thinning or insect and fire mitigation, the available woody biomass is smaller in diameter than commercial forest harvest. A study in the Western States found that most stems that were to be removed by fuel reduction treatments were < 2 inches in diameter. Eighty-six percent of the trees were < 10 inches in diameter, although they only accounted for 28 percent of the total volume (U.S. Department of Agriculture Forest Service 2003).

Forest resources within the WUI represent significant volumes. For example, Ku and Baker (1993) determined that in southern Arkansas and northern Louisiana the volume of biomass < 5.5 inches in diameter averaged 10.5 dry tons per acre, with no difference between winter and summer harvest. In their analysis, high density pine stands produced 53 percent more biomass than high density pine-hardwood stands.

On the other hand, economic feasibility is an issue. A 1992 study reported that only 40 percent of the hardwood inventory in Tennessee was economically available (Perlack and others 2005). However, if biomass is harvested and processed using integrated systems for merchantable products and biomass, economical recovery can be > 90 percent.

URBAN WOOD WASTE

As the U.S. landscape evolves, the amount of forest land within the WUI increases. However, traditional forestry practices may not be widely accepted in these areas because average tract sizes are small and harvesting results in close contact with neighboring residents. If neighbors object to certain harvesting techniques or prescribed burning, different management approaches to land management and woody biomass collection will be required. In addition to forest plantations within the WUI, woody biomass is also generated from tree and yard trimmings, commercial tree care industry, utility line clearings, and green space maintenance. Some of this material enters the solid waste stream, while other portions are handled by the generator or at its origin.

Urban wood waste is a significant woody biomass resource. One study estimated the annual volume of woody yard trimmings in the United States at 9.8 million dry tons annually, based upon an average moisture content of 40 percent (Perlack and others 2005). Another study on urban wood waste from 30 U.S. metropolitan areas determined that municipal solid waste (MSW) wood, industrial wood, and construction/demolition (C/D) debris averaged 666 pounds per person per year. Several southern cities were included in the study, and generation rates in the Southern United States varied from a low of 494 pounds per person per year (Florence, SC) to a high of 1,504 pounds per person per year (Richmond, VA) (Wiltsee 1998).

The U.S. Environmental Protection Agency reported that 28.6 million tons of yard trimmings (vegetative material that enters the solid waste stream from residential, commercial, and institutional sources, excluding C/D debris) were generated in the United States in 2003, representing 12 percent of the total U.S. MSW and equating to an average of about 190 pounds of trimmings per person per year (based on 2003 population figures) (U.S. Environmental Protection Agency 2005).

The amount of yard trimmings generated within each community varies significantly. Using 2000 population figures and State MSW data, Florida's yard trimmings were 14 percent of its total MSW and averaged 452 pounds per person per year. In contrast, Virginia's yard trimmings were only 4 percent of its total MSW, amounting to about 221 pounds per person per year (Commonwealth of Virginia 2002, Florida Department of Environmental Protection 2003, U.S. Census Bureau 2005). Nationally, in 2003 about 56 percent of yard trimmings were recycled, most of which was composted (U.S. Environmental Protection Agency 2005).

Yard trimmings consist of tree trimmings, grass clippings, garden wastes, prunings, leaves, Christmas trees, and the wood waste and paper component of domestic garbage (Sims 2002). The material from residential curbside and commercial landscaping sources often is dominated by smaller, higher moisture material. A study of curbside-collected yard trimmings in Florida found that most of the material (by weight) was grass clippings (**fig. 2.4A**) (Florida Organics Recyclers Association 1996).

Grass clippings and smaller trimmings from shrubs generally have higher moisture content (often > 50 percent) and levels of soil contamination than do larger diameter woody material. However, grass and leaves also contain higher levels of degradable carbohydrates and are more suitable for composting or other biodegradation. People tend to bring more woody material to central dropoff locations instead of leaving them curbside (**fig. 2.4B**) (Florida Organic Recyclers Association 1996). Material of this type has been found to have a moisture content of about 45 percent and fairly low levels of soil contamination (Atkins and Donovan 1992) as compared to curbside-collected material. However, larger material was also more likely to have large pieces of contamination such as scrap metal, rock, or concrete, and these contaminants present processing difficulties.

In addition to yard trimmings, trees and tree debris are generated by line clearing, right-of-way maintenance, and green space maintenance by utility companies and local governments. This material contributes to the biomass harvest from the urban forest but sometimes does not enter the MSW stream. A 1994 study found that an estimated 56,000 arboriculture and urban forest industry firms exist in the United States (NEOS 1994). These municipal and commercial tree care firms generated an estimated 200 million cubic yards of material (**fig. 2.5A**), with residues distributed similarly to those of Florida, which are displayed in figure 2.4A. Residues generated by these firms are often difficult

to dispose of, and survey results showed that 42 percent of this material was given away (**fig. 2.5B**).

Many State legislatures have banned the disposal of tree and landscape residue in landfills, increasing the cost of disposal. The high cost of disposal (tipping fees) at most MSW landfills has forced many commercial tree companies to seek alternatives for handling the woody biomass generated in their operations. In some locations, logs are occasionally removed from the urban wood stream and marketed to wood products manufacturers, as some tree species yield economic returns of two to four times more in lumber than firewood (Cesa and others 1994). However, metal in logs, e.g., from wires and nails, reduces sawmill demand for these logs.

Natural disasters also generate considerable woody debris. Seventy-eight percent of natural disaster woody material comes from wind storms, and 16 percent from ice storms or freezes. Of the material generated from natural disasters, 97 percent of the volume is generated in municipal areas with populations > 100,000. Seasonally, about 58 percent of the volume was produced in the summer and fall, and about 42 percent in the winter and spring (NEOS Corp. 1994).

In addition to the material generated by the urban forest industry, some urban wood waste ends up classified as C/D debris because site conversion and land clearing often is accompanied by new construction. C/D debris can vary from as low as 15 to as high as 85 percent wood, depending upon the source of the waste and where in the solid waste stream the wood is measured (Atkins and Donovan 1992). However, C/D debris is also often

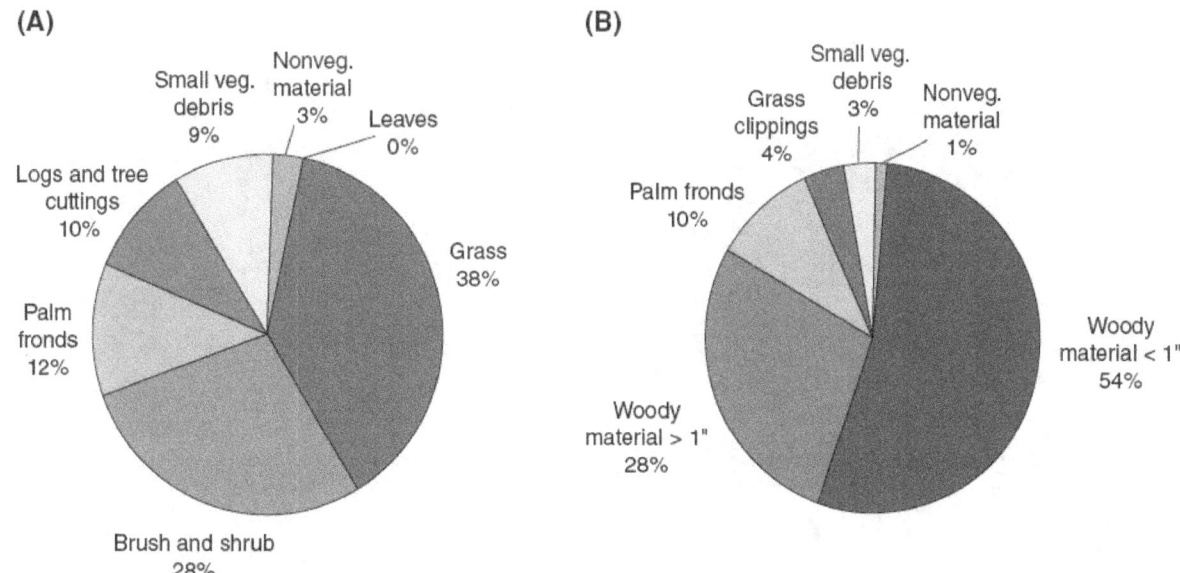

(A)

- Nonveg. material 3%
- Small veg. debris 9%
- Leaves 0%
- Logs and tree cuttings 10%
- Palm fronds 12%
- Grass 38%
- Brush and shrub 28%

(B)

- Small veg. debris 3%
- Grass clippings 4%
- Nonveg. material 1%
- Palm fronds 10%
- Woody material < 1" 54%
- Woody material > 1" 28%

Figure 2.4—Percent of total weight of curbside-collected yard trimmings (A), and yard material brought to central dropoff locations in Florida (B) (adapted from Florida Organic Recyclers Association 1996).

contaminated with paint, preservatives, and other substances that may be harmful to the environment if burned or otherwise used directly for bioenergy. These materials may require special processing to ensure that additional pollution does not result from their use as fuel.

EXOTIC PLANT REMOVALS, NATIVE PLANT RESTORATION, AND LAND CONVERSION

Exotic plant eradication programs are another recurring source of biomass for bioenergy. Issues related to invasive plant species are increasing in the WUI as human influences and human-induced disturbances increase. Harvesting for fuelwood can also be integrated into restoring degraded or high-graded lands or for native plant restoration projects (Andersson and others 2002). In the Southern United States, bioenergy markets could facilitate ongoing longleaf pine restoration programs by reducing costs for land clearing, hardwood control treatments, and site preparation. Conversion of forest lands for development also creates potential sources of biomass because lands slated for development in areas beyond hauling distance to mills are often clearcut and trees are either chipped and mulched or burned onsite for disposal.

SHORT-ROTATION INTENSIVELY MANAGED FORESTS

Demand for energy and bioproducts could present opportunities to develop dedicated bioenergy plantations. These plantations could produce biomass specifically for energy generation and to augment existing biomass resources, thus, ensuring adequate feedstock availability. Bioenergy plantations can be agricultural systems that produce herbaceous crops such as switchgrass

(Panicum virgatum), sugarcane *(Saccharum officinarum),* and others and they also can produce short-rotation woody crops (SRWC).

Ideal SRWC species grow quickly, produce high energy yields, and typically can coppice (regrow from the stump following harvest), which reduces replanting costs. Under coppice management, three to five growth stages can be harvested during the life of a tree, with each growth stage lasting 2 to 10 years. SRWC production largely resembles agriculture, often using adapted agricultural equipment to improve the efficiency of site preparation, planting, weed control, and harvest (Culshaw and Stokes 1995). SRWC plantations are operational in New York State and prevalent in Sweden and other parts of Europe. While SRWC plantations in the United States have been largely dedicated to the production of pulpwood (Culshaw and Stokes 1995), these plantations are likely to expand to meet future demand for renewable energy (Berndes and others 2003, Volk and others 2004).

In the United States, 22 hardwood species have been identified as potential SRWCs (Ranney and others 1986). Native species such as sweetgum *(Liquidambar styraciflua),* American sycamore *(Platanus occidentalis),* eastern cottonwood *(Populus deltoides),* and hybrid poplars *(Populus* spp.) are well adapted to the South, yielding 3 to 5 dry tons per acre per year. Exotic candidates for the subtropical South (Florida, Puerto Rico, and the U.S. Virgin Islands) include *Eucalyptus* spp., with the potential for exceptional yields of over 9 dry tons per acre per year (Klass 1998), and *Leucaena leucocephala,* a multipurpose tree with the potential to fix nitrogen and produce forage for livestock. *Eucalyptus grandis* has been produced commercially in southcentral Florida

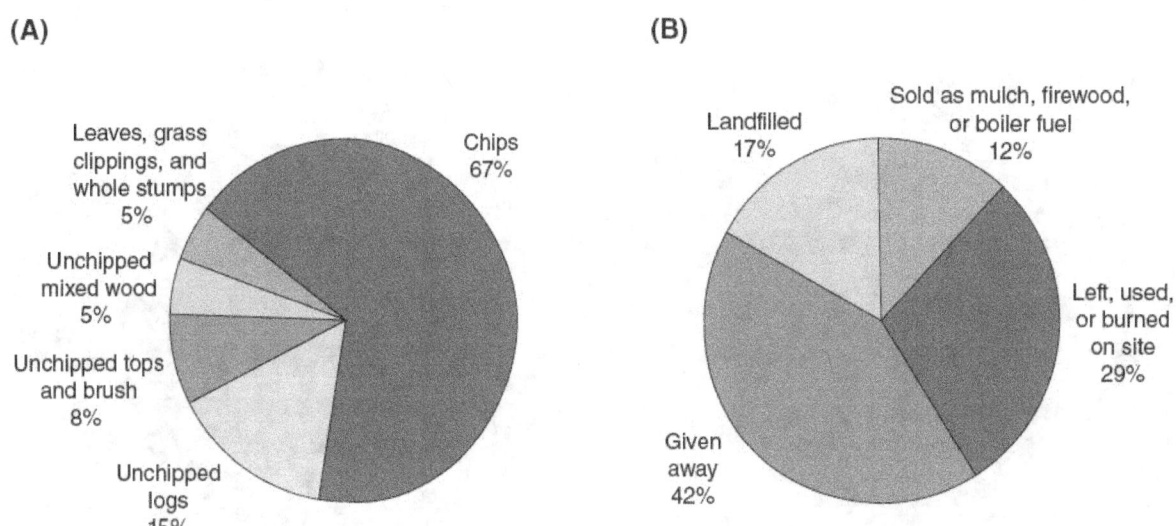

Figure 2.5—Amounts collected by U.S. urban forestry firms by material type (A), and disposal method (B) [adapted from NEOS (1994) survey of 1,330 respondents].

since the 1970s without spreading (Rockwood 1996), and *L. leucocephala* is available in sterile varieties; however, past and current problems with encroachment of invasive exotic species may mean easier public acceptance with native species.

SRWC production systems can be designed and implemented to provide not only local environmental services within the WUI but also biomass production. For example, SRWC plantations can be irrigated with municipal wastewater or fertilized with treated biosolids or municipal compost, simultaneously increasing biomass production, reducing fertilizer costs, and intercepting nitrates and phosphates to reduce nutrient loading in waterways (e.g., Aronsson and Perttu 2001, Rockwood and others 2004).

Although dendroremediation-produced biomass often contains heavy metals, cofiring dendroremediation-produced biomass with coal is cleaner than firing coal alone (Licht and Isebrands 2005). Gasification of contaminated biomass can be optimized to concentrate heavy metals in a small ash fraction for proper handling (Vervaeke and others 2005).

SRWC can also help build soil organic matter, recycle nutrients, and maintain vegetative cover to restore ecological functions on mined lands and other degraded lands (Bungart and Huttl 2001, Stricker and others 1993). SRWC established on agricultural lands as shelterbelts or buffer zones to protect riparian areas often reduce soil erosion and runoff of agricultural inputs, as well as improve wildlife habitat (Joslin and Schoenholtz 1997, Thornton and others 1998, Tolbert and Wright 1998).

Though SRWC plantations do not provide all the environmental services of a less intensively managed forest, e.g., wildlife enhancement values associated with forest structural diversity, opportunities exist to apply these systems within a mosaic of other land uses and to land that might otherwise not be used, while providing beneficial environmental services and producing bioenergy feedstocks.

WOOD AS A FUEL

The fuel quality of WUI forest biomass used as a bioenergy resource is determined by its physical characteristics. These characteristics—based on the relative contribution of leaves, needles, branches, stem, bark, soil contamination, and moisture content—can be influenced to varying degrees. For example, moisture content can be lowered by drying, and bulk density is a function of the size and other physical characteristics of the wood pieces. Volatile matter and the chemical composition also influence the energy content of the wood, commonly measured in Btus. Ash, the mineral content of the fuel, originates both from naturally occurring minerals in woody biomass and from contamination by soil. Boiler designs consider the ash content of the fuel, balancing heat protection for the grate and costly outages due to slagging and fouling (Sims

2002). Wood ash from combustion plants can also be reapplied to forest lands, so that some of the nutrients removed during harvest can return to the soil.

CONCLUSIONS

Woody biomass in the WUI is dispersed in a variety of forms across the landscape, making the availability of woody biomass difficult to predict. Woody biomass feedstocks tend to change over time due to changes in wood processing technologies, e.g., mill residues, harvesting technologies, landscape patterns, and market competition for the material.

As discussed in chapter 3, the nature of the feedstock (high moisture content, variable ash content, high volatiles and relatively low caloric content, and variable size and shape) requires careful consideration in the design of harvesting, handling, and conversion systems. These systems are intimately connected to the source of woody biomass, as is the decision for the enduse of woody biomass and, ultimately, the amount and type of power generated from it (see chapter 4). The more consistent the feedstock, the more closely the handling system and conversion plant can be matched to it for greater overall efficiency of the plant and to avoid the extra cost associated with overengineering the system to handle variable feedstocks (Sims 2002).

As discussed in chapter 5, the quantity and quality of biomass vary greatly by location and season. Its delivered price will be determined by such factors as where woody biomass originates, how much is available, collection and transportation equipment employed, and the quality of feedstock. Within the WUI, woody biomass is generated from forestry and forest management activities, urban activities, and potentially dedicated biomass operations. Increased demand for woody biomass generated by a bioenergy market may increase biomass prices, offsetting costs of thinning operations and enhancing opportunities for landowners to manage for higher value forest products.

Locating, collecting, and securing woody biomass from the WUI can be logistically challenging, and strategic planning should consider the future directions of development and land cover conversion, as well as public perceptions of woody biomass utilization (see chapter 7).

The development of plantations to specifically supply biomass and contributions from phytoremediation projects, which use trees and other vegetation to restore degraded land, provide opportunities to further increase woody biomass supplies. These residues—consisting of tree parts such as branches and tops and sometimes whole trees that are not considered saleable—are often left onsite after harvesting operations. Many stands, especially hardwood stands previously degraded from poor logging practices, may be dominated by low quality and low-value timber suitable for energy production. In some cases, removal of this low-value timber as biomass enables landowners to manage for higher quality future timber products.

To make appropriate design and scale decisions for conversion plants and handling systems for bioenergy projects, consideration of the quantity and quality of woody biomass resources available should be incorporated into the initial planning stage. These decisions impact every facet of a bioenergy project, from harvesting and conversion technologies to economic and social impacts. Careful consideration of the source of woody biomass will lead to more efficient use of this valuable natural resource.

REFERENCES

Alig, R.; Mills, J.; Butler, B. 2002. Private timberlands: growing demands, shrinking land base. Journal of Forestry. 100(2): 32–37.

Andersson, G.; Asikainen, R.; Björheden, R. [and others]. 2002. Production of forest energy. In: Richardson, J.; Björheden, R.; Hakkila, P. [and others], eds. Bioenergy from sustainable forestry: guiding principles and practice. The Netherlands: Kluwer Academic Publishers: 49-123.

Aronsson, P.; Perttu, K. 2001. Willow vegetation filters for wastewater treatment and soil remediation combined with biomass production. Forest Chronicle. 77(2): 293–299.

Atkins, R.S.; Donovan, C.T. 1992. Wood products in the waste stream; characterization and combustion emissions. Rep. 92–8. Albany, NY: New York State Energy Research and Development Authority. 4 p.

Berndes, G.; Hoogwijk, M.; van den Broek, R. 2003. The contribution of biomass in the future global energy supply: a review of 17 studies. Biomass and Bioenergy. 25(1): 1–28.

Bungart, R.; Huttl, R.F. 2001. Production of biomass for energy in post-mining landscapes and nutrient dynamics. Biomass and Bioenergy. 20(3): 181–187.

Cesa, E.T.; Lempicki, E.A.; Knotts, J.H. 1994. Recycling municipal trees, a guide for marketing sawlogs from street removals municipalities. NA-TP–02–94. Morgantown, WV: U.S. Department of Agriculture Forest Service, Northeastern Area, State and Private Forestry, Forest Resources Management. 49 p.

Commonwealth of Virginia. 2002. Solid waste managed in Virginia during calendar year 2001. Richmond, VA: Department of Environmental Quality. 8 p.

Culshaw, D.; Stokes, B. 1995. Mechanization of short rotation forestry. Biomass and Bioenergy. 9(1–5): 127–140.

Farnsworth, A.; Summerfelt, P.; Neary, D.G.; Smith, T. 2003. Flagstaff's wildfire treatments: prescriptions for community involvement and a source of bioenergy. Biomass and Bioenergy. 24(4–5): 269–276.

Florida Department of Environmental Protection. 2003. Solid waste management in Florida 2001-2002. Tallahassee, FL: Bureau of Solid and Hazardous Waste. 105 p.

Florida Organic Recyclers Association. 1996. Recycling yard trash: best management practices manual for Florida. Tallahassee, FL: Florida Department of Environmental Protection. 103 p.

Hakkila, P.; Parikka, M. 2002. Fuel resources from the forest. In: Richardson, J.; Björheden, R.; Hakkila, P. [and others], eds. Bioenergy from sustainable forestry: guiding principles and practice. The Netherlands: Kluwer Academic Publishers: 19-48.

Haynes, R.W. (tech. coor). 2003. An analysis of the timber situation in the United States: 1952 to 2050. Gen. Tech. Rep. PNW–GTR–560. Portland, OR: U.S. Department of Agriculture Forest Service, Pacific Northwest Research Station. 254 p.

Johnson, T.; Steppleton, C. 2005. Southern pulpwood production, 2003. Resour. Bull. SRS–101. Asheville, NC: U.S. Department of Agriculture Forest Service, Southern Research Station. 38 p.

Joslin, J.D.; Schoenholtz, S.H. 1997. Measuring the environmental effects of converting cropland to short-rotation woody crops: a research approach. Biomass and Bioenergy. 13(4–5): 301–311.

Klass, D.L. 1998. Biomass for renewable energy, fuels, and chemicals. San Diego: Academic Press. 651 p.

Ku, T.T.; Baker, J.B. 1993. Understory biomass from southern pine forests as a fuel source. In: Proceedings, first biomass conference of the Americas: energy, environment, agriculture, and industry. Golden, CO: National Renewable Energy Laboratory. 1: 284.

Licht, L.A.; Isebrands, J.G. 2005. Linking phytoremediated pollutant removal to biomass economic opportunities. Biomass and Bioenergy. 28(2): 203–218.

NEOS Corporation. 1994. Final report, urban tree residues: results of the first national inventory. Prepared for International Society of Arboriculture Research Trust. Savoy, IL. 65 p.

Perlack, R.; Wright, L.; Turhollow, A.F. [and others]. 2005. Biomass as feedstock for a bioenergy and bioproducts industry: the technical feasibility of a billion-ton annual supply. ORNL/TM–2005/66. Washington, DC: U.S. Department of Energy; U.S. Department of Agriculture Forest Service. 73 p.

Ranney, J.; Trimble, J.; Wright, L.; Perlack, R. 1986. Research on short-rotation woody crops in the South. New York: Third southern biomass energy conference: 71–79.

Rockwood, D.L. 1996. Using fast-growing hardwoods in Florida. Gainesville, FL: Florida Cooperative Extension Service. 8 p.

Rockwood, D.L.; Naidu, C.; Segrest, S. [and others]. 2004. Short-rotation woody crops and phytoremediation: opportunities for agroforestry? In: Nair, P.K.; Rao, M.R.; Buck, L.E., eds. New vistas in agroforestry, a compendium for the 1st World Congress of agroforestry 2004. Dordrecht, The Netherlands: Kluwer Academic Publishers: 51–63.

Rummer, B.; Len, D.; O'Brien, O. 2004. Forest residues bundling project-new technologies for residue removal. Auburn, AL: U.S. Department of Agriculture Forest Service, Southern Research Station, Forest Operations Research Unit. 18 p.

Shindler, B.; Toman, E. 2003. Fuel reduction strategies in forest communities: a longitudinal analysis of public support. Journal of Forestry. 101(6): 8–15.

Sims, R.E.H. 2002. The brilliance of bioenergy in business and in practice. London: James & James. 198 p.

Sims, R.E.H.; Bassam, N.E. 2003. Biomass and resources. In: Sims, R.E.H., ed. Bioenergy options for a cleaner environment. Amsterdam: Elsevier: 1-28.

Smith, W.; Miles, P.; Vissage, J.; Pugh, S. 2004. Forest resources of the United States, 2002. Gen. Tech. Rep. NC–241. St. Paul, MN: U.S. Department of Agriculture Forest Service, North Central Research Station. 137 p.

Stokes, B.; Siroios, D. 1989. Recovery of forest residues in the Southern United States. In: Stokes, B.J., ed. Harvesting small trees and forest residues: Proceedings of the International Energy Agency, task VI, activity 3 symposium. Auburn, AL: U.S. Department of Agriculture Forest Service, Southern Forest Experiment Station: 32–43.

Stricker, J.; Prine, G.; Anderson, D.L. [and others]. 1993. Production and management of biomass/energy crops on phosphatic clay in central Florida. Circ. 1084. Gainesville, FL: University of Florida. Florida Cooperative Extension Service. 8 p.

Thornton, F.C.; Joslin, J.D.; Bock, B.R. [and others]. 1998. Environmental effects of growing woody crops on agricultural land: first year effects on erosion, and water quality. Biomass and Bioenergy. 15(1): 57–69.

Tolbert, V.R.; Wright, L.L. 1998. Environmental enhancement of U.S. biomass crop technologies: research results to date. Biomass and Bioenergy. 15(1): 93–100.

U.S. Census Bureau. 2005. State and county quick facts. http://quickfacts.census.gov/qfd/. [Date accessed: July 18, 2006].

U.S. Department of Agriculture Forest Service. 2002. Timber product output database. http://srsfia2.fs.fed.us/php/tpo2/tpo.php. [Date accessed: November 15, 2005].

U.S. Department of Agriculture Forest Service. 2003. A strategic assessment of forest biomass and fuel reduction treatments in Western States. Washington, DC. 18 p.

U.S. Department of Agriculture Forest Service. 2004. Southern forest resource assessment, 2004. http://www.srs.fs.usda.gov/sustain/. [Date accessed: July 18, 2006].

U.S. Department of Agriculture Forest Service. 2005. Timber products output mapmaker. Version 1.0. http://ncrs2.fs.fed.us/4801/fiadb/rpa_tpo/wc_rpa_tpo.ASP. [Date assessed: July 18, 2006].

U.S. Environmental Protection Agency. 2005. Municipal solid waste. http://www.epa.gov/msw/facts.htm. [Date accessed July 18, 2006].

Vervaeke, P.; Tack, F.M.G.; Navez, F. [and others]. 2005. Fate of heavy metals during fixed bed downdraft gasification of willow wood harvested from contaminated sites. Biomass and Bioenergy. 30(1): 58–65.

Volk, T.; Verwijst, T.; Tharakan, P. [and others]. 2004. Growing fuel: a sustainability assessment of willow biomass crops. Frontiers in Ecology and the Environment. 2(8): 411–418.

Wear, D.; Carter, D.; Prestemon, J. 2005. The US South's timber sector in 2005: a prospective analysis of recent change. Gen. Tech. Rep. SRS–99. Asheville, NC: U.S. Department of Agriculture Forest Service, Southern Research Station. 29 p.

Wear, D.; Greis, J. 2002. The southern forest resource assessment - summary report. Gen. Tech. Rep. SRS–54. Asheville, NC: U.S. Department of Agriculture Forest Service, Southern Research Station. 103 p.

Wiltsee, G. 1998. Urban wood waste resource assessment. NREL/SR-570-25918. Golden, CO: National Renewable Energy Laboratory. 227 p.

Wolfe, R. 2000. Research challenges for structural use of small-diameter round timbers. Forest Products Journal. 50(2): 21–29.

Xu, W.; Carraway, B. 2005. Biomass from logging residue and mill residue in east Texas, 2003. College Station, TX: Texas Forest Service. 10 p.

Glossary of Terms

C/D debris: debris generated from construction or demolition of structures. C/D debris may contain land clearing urban wood waste removed in the process of new construction.

coppice: the ability of a tree to regrow from the stump after harvest.

forest residue: the aboveground materials generated from logging during precommercial thinnings and harvesting operations, e.g., leaves, bark, tops, and broken trees.

hardwood: angiosperm tree species that are characterized by broad leaves (as opposed to needles) and are usually deciduous.

landing: the site where logs are accumulated for loading on to trucks during a harvest operation.

logging residue: poor quality trees and tree components, such as crowns and stump-root systems that are left onsite during commercial harvesting operations.

merchantable timber: trees which are economically valuable to harvest.

Mg: megagram = 106 kilograms.

MSW: municipal solid waste collected from residences, commercial businesses, and governmental agencies and delivered to solid waste facilities for disposition or recycling. Urban wood waste, yard trimmings, and C/D debris may be considered MSW if these materials are collected, handled, and delivered to permitted solid waste facilities.

nonindustrial private landowner: a person owning < 1,000 acres of forested land who is not directly affiliated with a wood processing plant.

nonmerchantable timber: trees which are not harvested because they are too small, poor quality, or are not an economically valuable species.

phytoremediation: the use of trees or other vegetation to remove contaminants, such as heavy metals, and restore degraded land.

pulpwood: trees and wood suitable for manufacturing paper; purified cellulose products, such as absorbents, filters, rayon, and acetate; and oleoresin products, such as pine oils, fragrances, cosmetics, and thinners (www.sfrc.ufl.edu/Extension/ssfor11.htm).

sawtimber: trees that meet minimum diameter and stem quality requirements, making them suitable for conversion to lumber.

skidding: moving trees from a felling site to a loading area or landing, usually using specialized logging equipment.

slagging and fouling: the formation of deposits on boiler tubes, usually due to the presence of chemical contaminants.

softwood: coniferous tree species that are characterized by needlelike leaves, and are usually evergreen.

SRWC: short-rotation woody crops.

stumpage: the price paid by buyers to landowners for standing timber.

tipping fee: an amount paid to dispose of waste.

WUI: wildland-urban interface.

Chapter 3

Harvesting, Preprocessing, and Delivery of Woody Biomass in the Wildland-Urban Interface

Richard M. Schroeder

INTRODUCTION

Management of timber resources in the wildland-urban interface (WUI) is challenging, particularly with regard to fire control and product utilization. This chapter considers some of the issues associated with harvesting, preprocessing, and delivery of woody biomass in the WUI; explores the relationship of harvesting to fire control; reviews various harvesting systems; and examines related topics, including environmental impacts and regulatory issues. The objective is to provide land managers with information on methods available to harvest and transport woody biomass in the WUI.

To derive maximum use of forest resources generated within the WUI, harvesting, processing, and delivery methods compatible with unique WUI characteristics must be developed. In some respects, these methods are similar to conventional harvesting of commercial forests. The primary differences involve size and location of tracts and types of materials harvested. These differences present both challenges and opportunities for effective biomass recovery. Nevertheless, development of efficient biomass recovery systems in the WUI is critical because biomass materials can represent a low-cost source of renewable energy.

Within the WUI, wildfire hazard is a major concern, and harvesting and utilization of the excess woody biomass is one of several alternatives for reducing fuel buildup. Prescribed burning to reduce fuel buildup has been the most common practice in conventional forestry. In many parts of the South, the WUI is expanding into areas of vegetation, such as upland pine forests, which have naturally evolved to become dependent on wildfire for regeneration. Because these WUI areas are more accommodating to development and construction, the value of land near urban areas has increased, leading to higher population densities and more roads in formerly open rural areas. Higher population densities within these areas make it more difficult to plan, implement, and control prescribed burning. In addition, factors such as safety, liability risk, negative public perception, and smoke issues are making it more difficult for foresters to use prescribed fire as a land management tool. But without fire, hardwoods encroach, pines become overly dense, and fuels become abundant.

Where smoke issues are a concern, mechanical site treatment can reduce fuel materials. One form of mechanical treatment involves using specialized equipment that reduces fuel loads by grinding and mulching vegetation at the site (Mitchell and Rummer 1999, 2001; Rummer and others 2002; Thompson 2002). This method would be most cost effective when the resulting biomass material has no market potential and harvesting and transporting it would cost more than grinding in place (Stanturf and others 2003). Herbicides have been used to control undesirable understory vegetation in some managed forests. While useful in some areas of the WUI, herbicides are generally a high-cost option that may be perceived negatively by the public. Also, herbicides do not remove the fuel, which may increase fire hazard immediately after use.

HARVESTING WOODY BIOMASS

Some of the main factors that influence harvesting costs are the method used, stem size, material type, e.g., trees vs. residues, and amount of material removed (Hartsough and Stokes 1990). In general, harvesting costs per unit of material are lower with larger trees and higher volumes removed per ha (Holtzscher and Lanford 1997, Kluender and others 1997).

Another factor in harvest cost is tract size. Land in the WUI is often fragmented and noncontiguous, requiring harvest methods appropriate for smaller stands. Conventional forest harvesting operations are more costly as tract sizes fall below 10 ha (Rummer and others 1997), due, in part, to the high cost of moving, loading, and relocating mechanized equipment. For small tracts, the cost and efficiency of using manual labor for harvesting understory vegetation has also been studied. Because workers are not in enclosed equipment cabs, safety liability is a major impediment. However, such labor intensive systems, with their lower capital investment, can be the most cost effective, especially when conditions or volumes within a stand restrict productivity of large machinery (Bolding and others 2003).

Harvesting systems for pine and hardwood species often use the same machinery and techniques, with similar results. However, southern hardwoods are often located in lower, wetter areas. Consequently, less hardwood harvesting is likely to take place in the WUI. The exception is where undesirable hardwood understory is being removed. The discussion here generally applies to softwood and hardwood species. Harvesting systems, residue harvesting, and environmental issues surrounding harvesting of woody biomass are discussed in the following paragraphs.

Conventional Harvesting Systems

When considering harvesting within the WUI, existing and proven mechanized timber harvesting systems should be considered first. These systems have evolved for > 50 years to become the most efficient and least expensive method of removing volume from the forest. There are four primary functions that timber harvesting systems must accomplish: (1) felling; (2) processing (delimbing, bucking, topping); (3) intermediate transport (skidding or forwarding); and (4) loading (Wilhoit and Rummer 1999). Delimbing, cutting to length (bucking), and removing the top (topping) are not required when harvesting biomass, unless the log portion of the tree is to be separated. There can also be an additional step, size reduction (chipping or grinding), which is discussed later in this chapter.

Biomass harvesting systems normally involve removing the entire tree, whereas conventional harvesting systems generally focus on only the main stem. For this reason, equipment design and operation are somewhat different. Work in biomass harvesting in the 1980s focused on adapting existing systems to harvest conventional products, such as saw logs and pulpwood, as well as residues from logging operations (Stokes and Sirois 1989, Stokes and others 1984). Conventional harvesting equipment, such as feller bunchers and skidders, were complimented with whole-tree chippers, flail delimbers, and grinders that allowed particle size reduction and collection of nonmerchantable material. By 1992, several fuel harvesting systems were in operation. Most utilized feller bunchers (generally rubber-tired), grapple skidders, and large chippers that operated at the landing site (Stokes 1992). At some mills, whole trees were delivered to the mill sites using trailers modified to haul trees with the tops intact. At the mill, tops and limbs were removed and used for fuel. During the late 1990s, many of these systems were discontinued due to lower fuel prices.

Hartsough and others (1995) analyzed five conventional mechanized harvesting systems, four of which processed the nonmerchantable portion as biomass fuel. These systems represent the most common equipment scenarios currently available from existing logging contractors. Studies have consistently shown that the most economical method of harvesting biomass is the integration of existing harvesting operations and the collection of both merchantable material and biomass in a single pass (Greene and others 2006, Rummer 2006) Following are descriptions of harvesting systems used in the studies:

- Feller buncher-skidder-flail/chipper: Feller bunchers cut the trees, and skidders delivered them to one combination flail delimber-debarker-chipper, where the stems were debarked and then chipped into pulp-grade chips. In this scenario, the nonmerchantable material was not processed, and was left in the forest.

- Feller buncher-skidder-processor-loader-chipper: All material was felled with tracked feller bunchers that separated merchantable trees into separate piles as they were cut. The remaining biomass was lumped together into a second pile. The merchantable trees were skidded to a processor that mechanically delimbed, bucked, and topped the trees. Most of the limbs removed by the processor were left in the woods as they were cut or were returned to the woods by the skidders. The remaining material was taken to a chipper where it was processed for fuel.

- Harvester-forwarder-loader-chipper: This system utilized one harvester, a machine that processes (fells, delimbs, bucks, and piles) both biomass and saw-log trees in separate piles. A forwarder loaded both types of material and carried them to a landing. Saw logs were loaded with one conventional log loader, and the biomass was processed with a chipper. The chips were used for fuel.

- Feller buncher-harvester-skidder-loader-chipper: Merchantable trees were processed with one harvester, while the feller buncher cut biomass trees. Three skidders pulled both types of piles to a landing, where one conventional log loader loaded the saw logs and one chipper handled the biomass.

- Harvester-forwarder: In this system, only merchantable stems were harvested using harvesters and forwarders. The nonmerchantable biomass was left in the stand for this study, although this system could also be used to remove biomass in other applications.

Tract size may be one of the most important factors in cost of harvesting within the WUI. This was demonstrated in a cost-and-productivity study by the USDA Forest Service, Southern Research Station in 2005 in southern Alabama (Mitchell 2006). In an effort to enhance red-cockaded woodpecker habitat, small tracts of natural pine (Pinus spp.) were treated (in a manner similar to a fuel-reduction harvest) to remove the understory of small-diameter trees. Two 10-acre tracts were treated with conventional harvesting and chipping equipment. All trees < 7.5 inches in diameter were removed, with the average cut tree being < 3 inches in diameter. Researchers found that the operating cost of chipping biomass and transporting it nearly 60 miles was $11.44 per green ton, but the total cost of transportation, overhead, and profit was an additional $14 to $15 per green ton.

The systems described above are expensive, highly mechanized operations that require large volumes of material to be harvested each day to justify the expense. In 1995, the capital cost for each biomass handling system (systems 1 through 4) was estimated to be $1.2 to $2 million (Hartsough and others 1995). In the first four harvesting systems, from four to eight separate pieces of equipment were transported to each site (each requiring a tractor and trailer), significantly adding to overall costs and making them less cost effective for harvest of small- or low-volume tracts, such as those that are to be thinned (Willhoit and Rummer 1999).

One disadvantage of conventional, large-scale harvesting systems, is that individual machines often are designed to operate best under a limited variety of operating conditions. The WUI often contains a wide variety of conditions related to stand density, terrain slope, and average tree size. In the previously described conventional harvesting systems, as many as three skidders and two feller bunchers were sometimes required to keep up with one processor. The exception was the harvester-forwarder (system 5) or cut-to-length (CTL) system. The CTL system is often used in thinning or in sensitive areas where minimizing damage to residual trees is critical. In these situations, the CTL system causes less damage to residual trees than systems that remove longer trees. However, the CTL system is rarely used in clearcutting or in thinning plantations because it is generally more expensive than tree length operations.

Harvesting costs for the CTL system are greatly affected by tree size, especially if only the portion of tree suitable for pulpwood or saw logs is removed. On a weight basis, cost for harvesting trees 4 inches in diameter has been estimated to be 2 to 2.5 times more than harvesting 6-inch diameter trees, and more than 3 times the cost of harvesting 10-inch diameter trees (Holtzscher and Lanford 1997).

The CTL system has been combined with a small chipper to harvest biomass for energy (Bolding and Lanford 2001). In this operation, nonmerchantable trees are felled and piled during the harvest, along with limbs and tops from merchantable trees. A forwarder transports the nonmerchantable material to a chipper and the merchantable logs to log trailers. The chipper is smaller than traditional whole-tree chippers used in conventional harvesting systems, and more closely matched to the capacity of one harvester and one forwarder. For regenerated stands, the economics of the system include reduced site-preparation costs and the value of the material harvested in terms of energy content. In stands where biomass needs to be removed, the treatment value in reduced site-preparation costs can be 25 to 50 percent of the harvest value (Rummer 2006). Bolding and Lanford (2001) determined that the CTL approach was cost effective under a stand conversion scenario where site-preparation costs were a factor. This system

is quite capital intensive (estimated capital cost is $749,000), but fewer pieces of equipment and a smaller chipper make it more mobile than other conventional systems.

The previously described systems were based primarily on conventional logging equipment designed for large tracts of industrial forest. Over time, these conventional harvesting systems have become larger, more capital intensive, and better designed for large tracts of land. They also represent the systems commonly available to land managers considering harvesting within the WUI.

Small-scale Harvesting Systems

As demand for harvesting systems within the WUI increases, new systems better suited to small operations are being developed. Systems that employ machines with multiple functions will allow for fewer pieces of equipment and will be less expensive to move in and out of stands, so relocation will be more economical. Small equipment may be another consideration because more than one unit can be moved on a single large transport trailer (Stanturf and others 2003).

Small systems, such as the once common single-axle pulpwood truck and the manual chainsaw feller, are now rare in commercial pulpwood harvesting operations. Small-scale operations using manual chainsaw felling and either cable skidders or animals for skidding are still used for sawtimber harvests, especially in situations where volume is low, terrain is restrictive, or aesthetics are a major concern. Logging operations in urban areas of the Southern United States often use manual felling, trucks, and loading equipment designed for handling lengths cut for pulpwood.

Small and multiple-function equipment has been examined for use in biomass harvesting for several years. In analyzing the feasibility of using a multifunction machine, the fact that it can only perform one function at a time must be taken into consideration. In 1986, Stokes and Sirois evaluated a chipper-forwarder, which chipped wood in the field into an onboard container. The chips were transported in the container to a landing. Chipper-forwarders are not in common use in the United States today because of the relatively low value of the chips when used as fuel. However, they have been adopted in other parts of the world where higher fuel prices make the system more economical.

Efforts have been made to investigate new, small harvesting systems, often through modification of agricultural or industrial machines. Two primary objectives in developing small-scale timber harvesting systems are low capital investment and small physical size (Wilhoit and Rummer 1999). Because of low productivity and safety concerns, alternative small-scale systems must include mechanized felling and, preferably, mechanized processing as well. For optimum small-scale mechanized harvesting systems, the following machines should be considered:

- Four-wheel-drive farm tractors, small rubber-tire skid-steer machines, and larger rubber-track skid-steer machines
- Hydraulic shears for felling
- Harvester heads for processing, and
- Front loader or small knuckleboom attachments for loading

Today, many manufacturers are designing and manufacturing smaller scale harvesting equipment. In a recent trade publication, six manufacturers advertised harvesting attachments and carrier modifications for farm tractor or skid-steer machines, and nine manufacturers offered smaller scale chippers for use in timber harvesting (Forest Products Equipment 2005).

The use of livestock in timber harvesting systems (principally horses or mules) has nearly disappeared from commercial forestry in the United States. However, it may be reevaluated for use in some areas of the WUI where conventional harvesting equipment creates objectionable noise, traffic, or visual impacts. This method of harvesting may be more appealing to small landowners because it has lower impact during use and potentially causes less damage to residual trees.

Forest harvesting using animals is labor intensive. In addition, animal logging is perhaps more susceptible to interruptions by weather than mechanized logging. A 1999 study of animal (horses and/or mules) logging crews in northern Alabama found that, in general, animal loggers worked < 30 miles from home, and most moved their animals to the logging site each day and back home each night. The percentage of time spent working during a day ranged from 64 percent (owners) to 45 percent (crew members); the animals were only used 22 percent of the time (Wilhoit and Rummer 1999).

In countries with low labor costs, animal skidding for small-tree harvesting, particularly in thinning operations, is less expensive than machine skidding. This is not true for countries like the United States where labor costs are high. However, animal harvesting systems are less effective than machine skidding when the terrain is irregular and there is a high possibility of severe weather conditions. Long skidding distances are not conducive to the use of animals because of low ground speed (Wang 1999). Animal logging requires specialized support equipment and skilled and experienced operators (Rummer 1996). Such methods may be applied to the WUI, but success in using this type of operation will depend upon abilities of locally available contractors.

RESIDUE HARVESTING

Forest residue is the woody biomass left onsite after the harvesting of merchantable stand and tree components is complete. This is sometimes referred to as "logging slash" and is usually considered unsuitable for traditional products such as pulpwood or sawtimber (Stokes and Sirois 1989). Residue in the WUI may also include material generated from urban activities such as land clearing and tree debris generated from landscape maintenance, utility line clearance, and removal of tree debris from storms.

Two studies evaluated many of the available means and methods for recovery of forest residues, both in European and North American countries (Stokes 1992, Stokes and Sirois 1989). The studies indicated that conventional harvesting systems were most often used, and that grinding small pieces, such as tops and limbs at landings, was done using tub grinders and vertical feed hammer mills. These machines produce material with different particle sizes, which determines the amount of processing required at the end-user facility and may affect value of the delivered material. Particle sizing is discussed in the preprocessing section of this chapter.

In general, logging slash is less than one-quarter the density of solid wood (Rummer and others 2004) and weighs approximately 135 pounds per cubic yard (Rummer and others 2004). The productivity of any handling operation (hauling, skidding, and loading) is reduced by this low-density material, increasing harvesting and transportation costs per ton. The Florida Organics Recyclers Association (1996) estimates that the density of loose mixed brush generated from urban activities (which in many ways resembles conventional logging residue) is 100 to 250 pounds per

Removal of biomass as part of a conventional harvest is considered the most viable option in terms of cost and value. However, harvesting contractors question the impact on cost and productivity of adding a chipper and removing biomass during the harvest of conventional merchantable material. In a study using conventional equipment, biomass understory within a 33-year-old pine (Pinus spp.) plantation in southern Georgia was removed and chipped as part of a harvest of merchantable material (Greene and others 2006). Biomass included softwood and hardwood tops, branches, and undersized trees from 1 to 4 inches in diameter. About 15 green tons per acre of both tops and small trees were harvested. Results showed that daily production of roundwood was not decreased by the added production of biomass if at least 1 load of biomass could be harvested for every 10 loads of merchantable material.

cubic yard. This is probably representative of the southern region. In comparison, stacked pine pulpwood has a density of > 1,000 pounds per cubic yard.

Finding an effective method of densifying residues would reduce the cost of biomass collection. As early as 1987, the use of conventional round balers for collecting residues was examined by several researchers (Curtin 1987, Stokes and others 1987, Woodfin and Stokes 1987). These studies showed that while baling the residues was possible, the material sometimes needed to be crushed prior to baling (see preprocessing section of this chapter), and that bales often required hand feeding into the machine. To date, residue baling using conventional equipment has not been widely adapted.

Stokes and others (1987) reviewed a 1982 study that addressed increasing bulk density of loads of smaller diameter pieces harvested during thinning operations. Two experimental trailers were built that could compress the load using hydraulic compacting devices. In most cases, load compression was increased by 50 to 100 percent for softwoods and somewhat less for hardwoods. Results were better when low-moisture material such as field-dried biomass was used. However, transport costs for compressed loads on a per ton basis still tended to be higher because equipment costs were higher and the trailers were heavier, allowing less load capacity.

Much of the work dealing with machinery that compresses loose forest residues into uniform bundles has been done in Scandinavian countries. A bundling machine, coupled with a forwarder designed to handle the bundles, was tested in the Western States by the Forest Service (Rummer and others 2004). The bundler was a rubber-tired machine that collected, compressed, and bound forest residues into cylindrical bundles approximately 2 feet in diameter and 10 feet long. This simplified handling residues by compacting loose slash into a form that resembles a log. The forwarder then loaded the bundles and delivered them to a landing for transport. The study showed that such a system may be competitive with other forms of harvesting residue, but that the residues had to be properly placed on the ground to be effectively bundled.

ENVIRONMENTAL ISSUES

Harvesting operations, in general, have come under scrutiny and are the subject of controversy as a result of their adverse effects on the environment. Harvesting practices within the WUI can be expected to come under the same if not more scrutiny because they will often be more visible to the public.

Harvesting usually involves moving machinery or livestock teams over forested areas and removing biomass by cutting, lifting, and moving. Animal logging generally has less site impact than mechanized logging. The amount of machinery traffic on the site is a function of the intensity of harvesting. In a 1998 study of clearcut harvesting in loblolly pine plantations in northern Alabama, the use of Geographic Information System tracking on equipment showed that 25 percent of the stand incurred no traffic, 50 percent had one to five passes, and 25 percent had more than five passes. The number of passes was not clearly correlated with measured soil properties after the harvest (McDonald and others 1998).

When comparing harvesting methods such as single-tree selection, group selection, shelterwood, seed tree, and clearcuts, single-tree selection resulted in the most undisturbed soil area (39.4 percent) following harvest, while 9.1 percent of the seed tree and only 6 percent of the clearcut area remained undisturbed. Investigators reported that soil was most exposed in clearcut harvests (19 percent), followed by group selection (13.4 percent), shelterwood (13.3 percent), seed tree (12.7 percent), and single tree (11.8 percent) (Stokes and others 1995). Soil disturbance can result in higher levels of erosion, but exposed soil can be helpful in promoting natural regeneration, and can promote or accelerate the return of desirable species.

The environmental effects of biomass harvesting have not been extensively studied, but the impact may be similar to whole-tree harvesting, where entire trees with tops intact are removed and chipped. Whole-tree harvesting versus conventional stem harvesting has been studied for effects on nutrient losses and regrowth (Johnson and Todd 1987, Johnson and others 1988, Mann and others 1988, West and others 1981). Integrating biomass chipping and removal with the harvest of conventional products means that tops and branches normally left on the forest soil are removed from the site. A study conducted in slash pine plantations in southern Georgia examined what the total nutrient loss would be after harvest. Results indicated that if tops from all merchantable trees were removed, an additional 6.48 pounds of nitrogen, 0.52 pounds of phosphorus, and 1.73 pounds of potassium per acre would be removed, compared to harvesting only merchantable logs. When small trees (normally left behind) and tops from merchantable trees were removed, total nutrient losses were 24 pounds of nitrogen, 2.5 pounds of phosphorus, and 7.1 pounds of potassium per acre (Westbrook and others 2006).

Another Georgia study evaluated the effects that various site-preparation techniques had on nutrient losses when comparing conventional harvesting to whole-tree harvesting. Researchers found that in the southern Piedmont and Coastal Plain ecosystems, the method of site preparation had greater impact on nutrient losses than harvest method. Site-preparation techniques, especially the shear-pile-disk method, accounted for the highest loss of available nutrients, regardless of harvesting technique (Gaskin and others 1989).

Nutrient loss from any method of biomass harvesting may be offset by modifying site-preparation techniques to minimize soil disturbance and nutrient losses. On tracts of land where clearcutting and planting are practiced, if biomass harvesting can reduce the amount of residual material being handled during site preparation, less soil disturbance should take place, and the net effect on soil conditions and site productivity may actually be positive.

PREPROCESSING BIOMASS

To facilitate efficient transport, material handling, and utilization at the conversion facility, biomass is preprocessed during or after harvesting. The optimum treatment depends on characteristics of the material, the end use, and site-management requirements. In this discussion, preprocessing will address two critical characteristics of biomass: particle size and moisture content.

Particle Size

For nearly all end uses, ultimate material handling requires uniform particle size. Large-scale conversion facilities usually have additional sizing and classifying equipment onsite, but initial sizing often takes place prior to transport (exceptions include bundling of residues and transporting whole trees).

Particle sizing is often integral to biomass harvesting. Because of the diversity of biomass material taken from the WUI, some consideration of particle sizing technology is helpful. Forestry residues are usually processed to reduce the material size for economical removal, transport, and handling. Size reduction can assist in decreasing transport costs by increasing density of shipped material and decreasing air space in transported loads. Studies have shown that chipping of logging residues resulted in a 25-percent decrease in hauling costs (Stokes 1998).

There are still only a few commonly used methods to turn large pieces of woody material into small pieces. The following general categories of biomass size-reduction equipment can be used for comparison (Goldstein and Diaz 2005): chippers, which cut up material with a slicing action; grinders, which reduce particle size by repeatedly striking them with hammers or cutting heads; and shredders, which generally tear particles apart by shearing.

The most common size-reduction equipment in forestry is the chipper. Chippers are characterized by high output, high-speed cutting blades or knives. Most can also throw chips into transport trailers for hauling. Chipper knives must remain sharp and are susceptible to wear from high soil content, metal contamination, or rocks and stone. Because of this, when chipping dirty material, they require replacement and sharpening more often, which results in increased maintenance

and machinery downtime. Chippers are well integrated into existing harvesting systems because they are built to accept material of any length.

Grinders are types or derivatives of hammer mills, a type of machinery that evolved from milling processes for grains, meals, and powders. Forestry applications include horizontal feed grinders (material fed to hammers horizontally) and vertical feed grinders, such as tub grinders. Grinders are better at handling contamination than chippers, and they accept a wider range of piece sizes. Tub grinders are designed to take short, nonoriented pieces, including stumps, tops, brush, and large forked branches. Grinders rely on hitting a piece of wood (usually with high-speed rotating hammers) often enough to finally break it into the desired particle size. They require more energy than chippers per ton of output, and excessive soil can increase internal wear.

Shredders are generally slow-speed rip/shear devices used widely in tire shredding. Material is pinched between rotating devices and ripped apart or sheared. Shredders are useful when material is contaminated, e.g., with metal, rock, or concrete, because the internal parts are slow moving so damage to equipment can be avoided. Shredders are not used widely in biomass operations except as a first-stage size reducer because their capital cost is high and the particle size they produce is larger and less uniform than other options. Material from shredders usually requires further size reduction.

The desired particle size is determined by the buyer or end user. Generally, the size must be small enough to be conveyed using chain or belt conveyors, augers, or feed hoppers without interlocking or stringy pieces jamming the equipment. Typical conveying equipment used by the forest products and biomass combustion industries readily handles material that is < 3 inches in length. This can be accomplished with either chipping or grinding.

Moisture Content

Much of the biomass harvested for energy has been used as solid fuel for direct combustion, and the benefits of having drier fuel for this purpose are well documented. Dry fuel in a direct combustion boiler improves efficiency, increases steam production, reduces ancillary power requirements, reduces fuel use, lowers emissions, and improves boiler operation (Amos 1998).

Transpirational drying, also known as leaf seasoning, biological drying, and delayed bucking, occurs when felled trees are left in the forest for several weeks with the tops, branches, and leaves intact (Stokes and others 1993). The findings of some studies on transpirational drying are summarized below:
- In the upper Piedmont of Georgia, red oaks (Quercus rubra), sweetgum (Liquidambar styraciflua), and yellow poplars (Liriodendron tulipifera) were dried with tops intact for up to 8 weeks. Most moisture loss occurred in the first 3 weeks.

Oaks had the least moisture loss, from 43 to 39 percent, and sweetgum had the highest moisture loss, from 54 to 39 percent (McMinn 1986).

- Drying 6-inch d.b.h. eucalyptus (*Eucalyptus* spp.) trees in Florida for 4 weeks resulted in moisture content reduction from about 55 to about 43 percent at the base of the tree, and from 55 to 38 percent at the top of the tree (McMinn and Stubbs 1985).
- Loblolly pine *(Pinus taeda)* trees 5 to 9 inches in diameter were dried for 2 weeks near Gainesville, FL. The moisture content was reduced from 52 to 48 percent (McMinn and Taras 1983).
- One of the few large-scale studies of transpirational drying was conducted in southern Alabama in 1987. Several hundred trees were felled for the study, and results were grouped by species, diameter, and drying time. Most drying occurred during the first 50 days (soft hardwoods dried within the first 30 days, and hard hardwoods within the first 40 days). Moisture contents after that period were about 37 percent for pine, 33 percent for soft hardwoods, and 32 percent for hard hardwoods (wet weight basis) (Stokes and others 1987).

Transpirational drying is important from the standpoint of transport costs and combustion efficiency. Typically loads reach maximum legal weight limits before they are filled to their maximum volumes. Thus, using drier and lighter wood usually allows a load to carry a greater volume of wood per load and more wood per load on a dry weight basis. This reduces the transport cost per unit of wood, as well as the amount of water being handled, transported, and evaporated through combustion.

Additional research was performed on a prototype roller crusher. This machine was designed to crush round, small-diameter stems and facilitate drying by opening the wood to transpirational drying. Results indicated that crushing facilitated drying during periods when rain was absent and that most drying was completed in the first 5 weeks after treatment. However, the study found no guaranteed benefit from crushing trees to increase the rate of moisture loss over long drying periods or during times of heavy rainfall (Sirois and others 1991).

Another approach to drying involves leaving chipped material in the woods prior to shipping. Storing biomass in piles presents problems not always found in piling other material such as clean pulpwood chips. Bark and foliage in the biomass greatly increase the rate of deterioration. In one study, chips from whole trees developed much more heat in a pile than clean wood chips, and decay rates for mixed hardwood chips in an outside pile were reported to be three times that for clean, debarked chips (Springer 1980). In addition, piling of chipped green biomass can lead to other problems in the WUI. Moving of chip piles by operators can result in generation of dust that is harmful to operators. Mulch and composting operators have reported the presence of molds or fungi in piles, e.g., *Aspergillus* spp., that may pose respiratory health

risks. Piles can also develop sufficient heat to present a potential hazard from spontaneous combustion. In addition, the cost of returning equipment to load biomass piles at a different time than the harvest leads to higher overall delivered costs.

Biomass drying can also be accomplished after delivery to the processing or conversion facility. In many cases, these facilities generate heat through combustion for electrical generation or other purposes. This often results in heat exhaust or excess low-pressure steam (waste heat) that can be used to further dry the material if the facility installs proper heat transfer equipment. The design and effectiveness of biomass drying through waste heat is dependent upon the particular conversion facility. Some processes, such as gasification or pyrolysis, benefit greatly from drier biomass, while other technologies, such as hydrolysis, may actually require high amounts of water to be effective. Consequently, the conversion facility makes decisions and capital investments regarding waste-heat drying. Further information about drying technology at conversion facilities is available in a review by Amos (1998).

DELIVERY METHODS

Most forestry products and harvested material are transported by truck. About 80 percent of the pulpwood delivered to U.S. mills in 1996 arrived by truck (McDonald and others 2001). Truck transport is usually the least expensive, but rail had a greater role in past years, particularly in large pulpmills or power plants with extensive rail facilities.

Biomass is almost always placed into a truck while in the forest, so the cost of handling and loading is already incurred. Rail and barge transportation require more handling of the biomass as material is moved from truck to barge or railcar and finally unloaded at the facility that will use it. These additional handling steps can add $3 or more per green ton to total freight costs. The cost per ton-mile for either rail or barge varies considerably and is dependent upon local availability. Because of added cost for extra handling, limited availability, and high variability in rail or barge freight rates, these options have a higher cost and are less efficient than trucking. Consequently, the remainder of this section will focus on truck transportation.

Transportation of conventional forest products accounts for about 25 to 50 percent of the cost of delivering materials to forest product mills, and this percent will likely increase as fuel prices escalate (McDonald and others 2001). Because biomass material has little to no value prior to harvest, the percentage of total cost in freight for biomass may be even higher than these values. Rummer (2006) concluded that transportation is the highest single component of total cost for delivering biomass.

Because transport makes up the largest portion of overall cost, studies have been conducted to increase transport efficiency. Locating, moving, loading, hauling, unloading, and returning transport vehicles are all logistical challenges for removing biomass material from the forest. Coordination between truck availability and rate of harvesting is important. The method of dispatching trucks to logging sites can affect productivity and associated costs, so trucking capacity must closely match logging capacity (McDonald and others 2001). Trucks with fixed-body lengths that do not pull trailers (and have removable rolloff pallet racks to supply small-scale users) have been tested, but results showed that more than one small-scale supplier may be needed to optimize the system (Rummer and Klepac 2003). Conventional trash rolloff containers have also been tested for hauling logging slash from harvesting sites in Montana. Results showed that coordination between the grinding, loading, and transport functions was critical to the economic feasibility of this method (Rawlings and others 2004).

Transport Equipment

The following is a review of transportation equipment likely to be used to move forest material in the WUI.

Trucks—As discussed, most biomass from the WUI is initially loaded into a truck and transported on existing roadways. Trucks for transporting commodities generally can be placed in one of two categories: fixed trucks and road tractors.

Fixed trucks are vehicles with a fixed cargo box, such as a local delivery truck or rental moving truck. Fixed trucks are for the most part < 40 feet in length, and the payload capacity is less than road tractors. Road tractors are designed to pull cargo trailers. These trucks are designed for greater capacity and offer the versatility of changing the type, size, and configuration of cargo space. Most goods in the Southern United States are currently transported in 80,000-pound gross vehicle weight (GVW) road tractor-trailer combinations.

Fixed trucks are usually shorter than road tractor-trailer combinations and allow more maneuverability in tight areas. Because of the lower payload capacity, fixed trucks are best when hauling distances are shorter.

Log or Bunk Trailers—This type of trailer is designed to haul trees, poles, or pulpwood in racks. They are lightweight and have high payload capacities. Residue bundles can also be transported in these types of trailers (Rummer and others 2004).

Vans—These tractor-trailer combinations are enclosed box trailers with their own axles and are most commonly seen transporting various types of cargo. Although some vans are watertight and even refrigerated, the ones used for transporting biomass are open at the top and not watertight.

Vans for forestry work are also known as "bulk vans" or "chip vans." Bulk vans have either an open end or an open top. Open-top bulk vans are usually loaded with front-wheel loaders from the side or from overhead bins. Open-end bulk vans are generally loaded directly from the rear by chippers that throw the material into the van. Depending upon weight of the road tractor and the trailer itself, a payload of about 42,000 to 52,000 pounds can be carried in most vans. For some cargo, volume capacity is more important than gross weight because the material is so light that, even when the vans are full, they may be carrying a payload less than the legal capacity. Most bulk vans carry between 100 and 135 cubic yards, although specialty chip vans for extremely light material, such as planer shavings, can hold 150 cubic yards or more.

Bulk vans can be unloaded using truck platforms that lift the truck and trailer and dump the material out the rear of the van, or by integral hydraulically operated self-unloading floors (called "live floors") that move the contents from inside to the rear and out of the tailgate. There are many advantages to self-unloading vans, including the flexibility of unloading in any location and the ability to handle a wide variety of loads. However, live-floor bulk vans are heavier than regular bulk vans, and this reduces the potential legal-weight capacity of the payload. Bulk vans are generally considered to be the most cost-efficient mode of transporting preprocessed biomass, but they are difficult to move into some harvesting areas because of poor road conditions. In these less accessible areas, other options such as container trailers should be considered (Rawlings and others 2004).

Container trailers—Container trailers handle most of the international trade that is moved by truck from ports, and this type of trailer also transports a large portion of the collected solid waste in the United States. The containers, which consist of a trailer chassis with a removable cargo box, vary in size, construction, and volume. The chassis can be designed to load and unload containers. Two common varieties are rolloff trucks or containers commonly used for collecting and hauling solid waste, and cargo trailers used for distributing goods from ships.

Container trailers are designed to hold bulk material and to be handled when fully loaded. They can be left on a site, filled as desired, and then removed and replaced with an empty container. Container trailers can also be used for storage of any delivered materials at the end user's site.

The distance from biomass site to handling facility and the time required for operation affect the cost of transportation. Inaccessible harvesting sites and inadequate unloading facilities are factors that can increase costs. Rummer (2006) estimated biomass transport costs of $3.50 to $4.50 per green ton for distances up to 40 miles and $0.12 to $0.15 per ton-mile for longer distances. The fixed amount for the first 40 miles reflects the lost time in loading and unloading.

REGULATORY ISSUES

Because of their closer proximity to more populated areas, WUI management activities are often more visible than conventional forestry operations conducted on large tracts or in remote areas. As a result, regulations regarding harvesting, preprocessing, and delivery may play a large role in developing appropriate practices for particular sites. Such regulations can impact landowner profits by increasing harvest costs and lowering stumpage prices (Spink and others 2000). They also can conflict with other regulations and ordinances.

In the South, local ordinances related to timber harvesting increased 345 percent from 1992 to 2000 and occurred in all Southern States except Kentucky, Oklahoma, and Tennessee (Jackson and others 2003). Ordinances generally fall into one of five categories: (1) environmental protection, (2) tree protection, (3) public property protection/safety, (4) timber harvesting, and (5) special feature protection. In a survey of 13 Southern States, protection of public roadways and public safety were the predominant objectives for timber harvesting regulations (Spink and others 2000). Timber harvesting ordinances, specifically restricting forestry and silvicultural operations, accounted for about 10 percent of the identified ordinances in 2000. Most of these contained requirements for management plans, harvesting permits, adherence to best management practices, and protection of streamside management zones. Ordinances in the category of public property protection also impact harvesting operations. These include load limits on roads, road damage, mud and logging debris, and restrictions against interfering with traffic flow. Special feature ordinances adopted to protect scenic or environmentally valuable areas were the next most common category and sometimes included tree cutting prohibitions and the requirement to obtain a cutting permit.

The number of regulations is increasing, as the survey revealed that of the 346 ordinances identified in the southern region, > 80 percent had been enacted in the last 10 years, and 44 percent in the last 5 years. In response to the many local ordinances, some Southern States have enacted "right to practice" laws. These laws are designed as mandates to ensure that forest landowners can continue to practice forestry. As of 2000, Kentucky, Virginia, and North Carolina had passed "right to practice" laws with varying levels of success (Spink and others 2000). In 2002, Georgia passed a law providing statewide consistency in county logging ordinances and set guidelines for counties to follow if they elect to enact local ordinances (Jackson and others 2003).

Within the WUI, local tree removal and tree protection ordinances related to tree size and tree replacement may be an issue to consider. Normally, most urban tree protection ordinances do not apply to forested areas in the WUI. However, when small, highly visible areas in the WUI are considered for harvesting, the local arboriculturist may become involved in the process.

Biomass for energy is often examined in the context of net energy gain, or energy balance. The amount of energy required to produce another unit of energy determines both the economic feasibility and the long-term practicality of any energy system. In a study of harvesting understory biomass, including tops and branches of harvested trees, Green and others (2006) determined that it took about 0.86 gallons of diesel fuel to harvest, chip, and load 1 green ton of biomass fuel at 50-percent moisture content. Assuming a freight distance of 30 miles and average payloads and fuel efficiency of 5 miles per gallon, an additional 0.24 gallons of diesel fuel was used to transport each ton. Thus, a total of 1.1 gallons of diesel fuel was consumed to harvest and deliver 1 green ton of biomass. If only the amount of diesel fuel used for harvest and transport is considered, and a green ton of biomass has a net heating value of 5,740,000 British thermal units (Btus), while a gallon of diesel fuel has a net heating value of 115,000 Btus, then biomass from the forest understory can produce > 45 times the net heating value of the diesel fuel it took to harvest and deliver it [fuel values from U.S. Department of Agriculture Forest Service (2004)]. Another study dealing with removal of understory in a natural longleaf pine (Pinus palustris) stand showed that the carbon harvested in fuel chips far offset the carbon used by fossil fuel consumption during harvest, resulting in a potential net carbon offset of 1.47 to 6.2 tons per acre harvested (Condon and Putz, 2007).

In addition to local and State regulations, the Federal Government regulates highway transportation. The applicable rules pertaining to truck size, truck weight, and route designations are the responsibility of the U.S. Department of Commerce and the U.S. Department of Transportation. Among other things, these rules specify the minimum restrictions that States can require on most improved highways that are partially funded with Federal highway money. In general, over-the-road tractor-trailer combinations can be up to 102 inches in width and 48 feet in length and have a total maximum weight of 80,000 pounds. States may enact width and weight limits that exceed the Federal standard. Most Southern States have adopted the legal minimum as their guidelines for legal loads, although weight and width restrictions are sometimes lifted for special circumstances, e.g., fire salvage and storm cleanup. The maximum weight is the GVW or the weight of both the payload and the vehicle. Transportation companies often spend more for lighter trucks and trailers because of their greater legal payload capacity.

Exceptions to weight and width limits can be made with special permits. These permits allow oversized loads to travel on the roads but limit their activities. In most Southern States, oversized vehicles are limited to traveling during daylight hours, and in some States, they cannot travel on holidays and weekends. These limitations often apply to vehicles moving harvesting machinery, thus adding to the cost of moving harvesting operations from one site to another.

In some jurisdictions, State and Federal incentives may be available for removal of understory as part of a forest health initiative or wildfire prevention strategy. The Forest Service or State forestry agency may help offset the cost of biomass removal to improve harvest feasibility, particularly in the WUI. These agencies will provide guidance on available funding and policies.

CONCLUSIONS

The biomass generated within the WUI is a potential source of renewable energy, especially for energy consumers in urban areas. Tops and branches from merchantable harvests, nonmerchantable timber trees, and understory vegetation all present opportunities for biomass accumulation, fire hazard reduction, increased stand productivity, and reduced site-preparation cost. Many variations of conventional harvesting systems have been tested, and combining biomass harvesting with conventional harvesting operations appears to be the most economical option.

The size of tracts that need to be treated in the WUI may be smaller than those normally harvested, which can greatly increase costs, especially if conventional harvesting equipment is used. Currently available equipment for transporting biomass from the WUI is the same as that used in conventional forestry operations. Innovation in transport methods, including increasing bulk density and use of transpirational drying, has the potential to make biomass harvesting from forest residues more attractive.

The environmental impact of biomass removal is a complex issue that requires further study. Initial research suggests that removal of biomass from the stand may not result in significant deterioration in soil properties or in nutrient loss, but data is limited.

Harvest of biomass fuel from forest residues, nonmerchantable timber, and urban tree debris may represent a significant opportunity to generate a substantial amount of net energy, because the net heating value of the biomass fuel produced greatly exceeds the fuel used in harvest and transport of the biomass materials. Managers considering harvest options for WUI stands should investigate local and State transportation regulations, as well as local ordinances that affect harvesting operations.

REFERENCES

Amos, W. 1998. Report on biomass drying technology. Natl. Renewable Energy Lab. Tech. Pap. 570–25885. Golden, CO: National Renewable Energy Laboratory. 28 p.

Bolding, M.C.; Lanford, B.L. 2001. Forest fuel reduction through energy wood production using a small chipper/CTL harvesting system. In: Wang, J.; Wolford, M.; McNeel, J., eds. Appalachian hardwoods: managing change: Proceedings of the 24th annual Council on Forest Engineering meeting. Corvallis, OR: Oregon State University: 65–70.

Bolding, M.C.; Lanford, B.L.; Kellogg, L.D. 2003. Forest fuel reduction: current methods and future possibilities. In: Proceedings of the 2003 Council on Forest Engineering. Bar Harbor, ME: [Publisher unknown]: 1–5.

Condon, B.; Putz, F. 2007. Countering the broadleaf invasion: financial and carbon consequences of removing hardwoods during longleaf pine savanna restoration. Restoration Ecology. 15: 2.

Curtin, D.T. 1987. Preliminary evaluation of conventional round baler for biomass recovery. Forest Energy Newsl. 7. Garpenberg, Sweden: Forest Energy Secretariat: 12–13.

Florida Organic Recyclers Association. 1996. Recycling yard trash: best management practices manual for Florida. Tallahassee, FL: Florida Department of Environmental Protection. 6 p.

Forest Products Equipment. 2005. St. Johnsbury, VT: MRP Publishing. 14(2). http://www.mrpllc.com/about.php. [Date accessed: January 29, 2010].

Gaskin, J.W.; Nutter, W.L.; McMullen, T.M. 1989. Comparison of nutrient losses by harvesting and site preparation practices. Georgia For. Res. Pap. 77. Atlanta: Georgia Forestry Commission: 1–6.

Goldstein, N.; Diaz, L.F. 2005. Size reduction equipment review. Biocycle. 46(1): 48.

Greene, W.D.; Westbrook, M.D.; Axler, R.L. 2007. Harvesting forest biomass by adding a small chipper to a ground-based tree-length southern pine operation. South. J. Appl. For. 31(4): 165–169.

Hartsough, B.R.; Stokes, B J. 1990. Comparison and feasibility of North American methods for harvesting small trees and residues for energy. In: Stokes, B.J., ed. Proceedings of the International Energy Agency, task VI, activity 3 workshop: harvesting small trees and forest residues. New Orleans: U.S. Department of Agriculture Forest Service, Southern Forest Experiment Station: 31–40.

Hartsough, B.R.; Stokes, B J.; McNeel, J.F.; Watson, W.F. 1995. Harvesting systems for western stand health improvement cuttings. In: Proceedings of the ASAE annual meeting. Pap. 95–7746. St. Joseph, MI: American Society of Agricultural Engineers: 1–8.

Holtzscher, M.L.; Lanford, B.L. 1997. Tree diameter effects on cost and productivity of cut-to-length systems. Forest Products Journal. 47(3): 25–30.

Jackson, B.; Hubbard, W.; Stringer, J.; Dillaway, D. 2003. A look at local and county ordinances that affect timber harvesting. Forest Landowner. 62(2): 42–46.

Johnson, D.W.; Kelley, J.M.; Swank, W.T. [and others]. 1988. The effects of leaching and whole-tree harvesting on anion-cation budgets of several forests. Journal of Environmental Quality. 17: 418–424.

Johnson, D.W.; Todd, D.E. 1987. Nutrient export by leaching and whole-tree harvesting in a loblolly pine and mixed oak forest. Plant and Soil. 102: 99–109.

Kluender, R.; Lortz, D.; McCoy, W. [and others]. 1997. Removal intensity and tree size effects on harvesting cost and profitability. Forest Products Journal. 48(1): 54–59.

Mann, L.K.; Johnson, D.W.; West, D.C. [and others]. 1988. Effects of whole-tree and stem-only clear-cutting on postharvest hydrologic losses, nutrient capital, and regrowth. Forest Science. 42: 412–428.

McDonald, T.; Carter, E.; Taylor, S.; Torbert, J. 1998. Relationship between site disturbance and forest harvesting equipment traffic. In: Proceedings of SOFOR GIS'98, 2d southern forestry conference. Athens, GA: University of Georgia: 85–92.

McDonald, T.; Taylor, S.; Rummer, R.; Valenzuela, J. 2001. Information needs for increasing log transport efficiency [CD–ROM]. In: First international precision forestry symposium. Seattle, WA: University of Washington. 12 p.

McMinn, J.W. 1986. Transpirational drying of Piedmont hardwoods. Georgia For. Res. Pap. 63. Atlanta: Georgia Forestry Commission. 7 p.

McMinn, J.W.; Stubbs, J. 1985. In-woods drying of eucalypts in southern Florida. Forest Products Journal. 35(11/12): 65–67.

McMinn, J.W.; Taras, M.A. 1983. Transpirational drying. In: Proceedings, 6th international Forest Products Research Society wood energy forum. [Place of publisher unknown]. [Publisher unknown]. 206–207.

Mitchell, D. 2006. Case study of a biomass chipping operation on national forest land. Presented at Smallwood '06 conference. [Place of publisher unknown]. [Publisher unknown] [Not paged].

Mitchell, D.; Rummer, B. 1999. Midstory reduction treatments with a Shinn SC-1. Tech. Release 99–R–29. Rockville, MD: American Pulpwood Association. 2 p.

Mitchell, D.; Rummer, B. 2001. Midstory reduction treatments with a Woodgator T-5. Tech. Release 01–R–15. Rockville, MD: Forest Resources Association, Inc. 2 p.

Rawlings, C.; Rummer, B.; Seeley, C. [and others]. 2004. A study of how to decrease the costs of collecting, processing and transporting slash. Missoula, MT: Montana Community and Development Center. 21 p. Available from: U.S. Department of Agriculture Forest Service, Southern Research Station, G.W. Andrews Forestry Sciences Laboratory, 520 Devall Drive, Auburn University, Auburn, AL 36849.

Rummer, B. 1996. Niche logging. Tech. Pap. 97–P–9. Rockville, MD: American Pulpwood Association. 5 p.

Rummer, B. 2006. Mechanized fuel reduction case studies. Presented at North Carolina wood energy conference. [Place of publisher unknown]. [Publisher unknown] [Not paged].

Rummer, B.; Carter, E.; Stokes, B.J.; Klepac, J. 1997. Strips, clear-cuts, and deferment cuts: harvest costs and site impacts for alternative prescription in upland hardwoods. In: Meyer, D.A., ed. Proceedings of the twenty-fifth annual hardwood symposium: 25 years of hardwood silviculture: a look back and a look ahead. Cashiers, NC: [Publisher unknown]: 103–112.

Rummer, B.; Klepac, J. 2003. Evaluation of roll-off trailers in small-diameter applications. In: Proceedings of the 2003 Council of Forest Engineering 26th annual conference. Bar Harbor, ME: University of Maine: 5 p.

Rummer, B.; Len, D.; O'Brien, O. 2004. Forest residues bundling project: new technology for residue removal. Internal report. Auburn, AL: U.S. Department of Agriculture Forest Service, Southern Research Station, Forest Operations Research Unit. 20 p.

Rummer, B.; Outcalt, K.; Brockway, D. 2002. Mechanical mid-story reduction treatments for forest fuel [Abstract]. In: Proceedings of new century: new opportunities: 55th annual Southern Weed Science Society meeting. Champaign, IL: Southern Weed Science Society: 76: 1.

Sirois, D.L.; Rawlings, C.L.; Stokes, B.J. 1991. Evaluation of moisture reduction in small diameter trees after crushing. Bioresource Technology. 37: 53–80.

Spink, J.J.; Haney, K.L., Jr.; Greene, J.L. 2000. Survey of local forestry-related ordinances and regulations in the South. In: Proceedings of the annual meeting of the Southern Forest Economics Workers. Monticello, AR: Arkansas Forest Resources Center: 41–46. Available from: U.S. Department of Agriculture Forest Service, Southern Research Station, G.W. Andrews Forestry Sciences Laboratory, 520 Devall Drive, Auburn University, Auburn, AL 36849.

Springer, E.L. 1980. Should whole-tree chips for fuel be dried before storage? FPL Res. Note FPL–0241. Madison, WI: U.S. Department of Agriculture Forest Service, Forest Products Laboratory. 6 p.

Stanturf, J.; Rummer, R.; Wimberly, M. [and others]. 2003. Developing an integrated system for mechanical reduction of fuel loads at the wildland/urban interface in the Southern United States. In: Proceedings of the 2^d forest engineering conference. Växjö, Sweden: Skogforsk: 135–138.

Stokes, B J. 1992. Harvesting small trees and forest residues. Biomass and Bioenergy. 2(1–6): 131–147.

Stokes, B J. 1998. Harvesting systems for multiple products an update for the United States. In: Wood fuels from conventional forestry: Proceedings of the 3rd annual workshop of activity1.2, task 7, international energy agency bioenergy task force. Auburn, AL: U.S. Department of Agriculture Forest Service, Southern Forest Experiment Station: 49–56.

Stokes, B J.; Kluender, R.A.; Klepac, J.F.; Lortz, D.A. 1995. Harvesting impacts as a function of removal intensity. Paper presented at XX IUFRO World Congress, P3.1 1.00, Forest Operations and Environmental Protection. Tampere, Finland: Forest Operations and Environmental Protection: 207–216.

Stokes, B J.; McDonald, T.P.; Kelley, T. 1993. Transpirational drying and costs for transporting woody biomass: a preliminary review. In: Proceedings of the IEA/BA task IX, activity 6: transport and handling. Aberdeen, United Kingdom: Aberdeen University: 76–91.

Stokes, B J.; Sirois, D.L. 1986. Evaluation of chipper-forwarder biomass harvesting concept. In: Rockwood, D.L., ed. Proceedings of the 1985 southern forest biomass workshop. Gainesville, FL: University of Florida, Institute of Food and Agricultural Sciences: 23–26.

Stokes, B.J.; Sirois, D.L. 1989. Recovery of forest residues in the Southern United States. In: Stokes, B J., ed. Proceedings of the International Energy Agency, task VI, activity 3 symposium: harvesting small trees and forest residues. New Orleans: U.S. Department of Agriculture Forest Service, Southern Forest Experiment Station: 32–43.

Stokes, B J.; Sirois, D.L.; Woodfin, S.L. 1987. Preliminary evaluation of steel-roller round baler for woody biomass baling. In: Proceedings of the 9th annual meeting of the southern forest biomass workshop. Starkville, MS: Mississippi State University, Department of Forestry: 167–174.

Stokes, B J.; Watson, W.F.; Miller, D.E. 1987. Transpirational drying of energy wood. ASAE Pap. 87–1530. St. Joseph, MI: American Society of Agricultural Engineers. 14 p.

Stokes, B J.; Watson, W.F.; Savelle, I.W. 1984. Alternate biomass harvesting systems using conventional equipment. In: Saucier, J.R., ed. Proceedings of the 1984 southern forest biomass workshop. Asheville, NC: U.S. Department of Agriculture Forest Service, Southeastern Forest Experiment Station: 111–114.

Thompson, J.D. 2002. Mulching machines for pre-commercial thinning and fuel reduction. Alabama's Treasured Forests. 21(2): 22–23.

U.S. Department of Agriculture Forest Service. 2004. Fuel value calculator. Publ. WOE–3. Madison, WI: U.S. Department of Agriculture Forest Service, Forest Products Laboratory, State & Private Forestry Technology Marketing Unit. 3 p.

Wang, L. 1999. Environmentally sound timber extracting techniques for small tree harvesting. In: Proceedings of the 1999 ASAE annual international meeting. ASAE Pap. 99–5053. St. Joseph, MI: American Society of Agricultural Engineers. 7 p.

West, D.C.; Mann, L.K.; Edwards, N.T. 1981. Whole tree harvesting; second year progress report-impacts on forest nutrient and carbon dynamics. ORNL/TM–7874. Oak Ridge, TN: Oak Ridge National Laboratory. 98 p.

Westbrook, M.; Greene, D.; Izlar, R. 2006. Harvesting forest biomass by adding a small chipper to a ground-based tree-length southern pine operation. In: Proceedings of the 2006 annual meeting of the council on forest engineering. Athens, GA: University of Georgia.: 1–25.

Willhoit, J.; Rummer, B. 1999. Application of small-scale systems: evaluation of alternatives. ASAE Pap. 99–5056. St. Joseph, MI: American Society of Agricultural Engineers. 18 p.

Woodfin, S.L.; Stokes, B J. 1987. Conventional round baler evaluated for biomass recovery. Biologue. 2(2): 8–9.

Glossary of Terms

bulk van: a type of trailer designed to transport bulk unpackaged goods, usually loaded from the top or from the rear.

bundler: a machine designed to lift forest residue, wrap pieces into a bundle, secure the bundle with twine, cut each bundle into desired lengths, and eject the bundle onto the ground.

chain flail debarker: a machine designed to remove branches and bark by passing stems through a series of high-speed swinging chains. Chain flail debarkers can include a loader or be loaded by another machine.

chipper: a machine, either stationary or mobile, designed to reduce tree stems or whole trees into wafer-shaped pieces or chips, using sharp knives.

chip van: a type of bulk van designed to transport forest products, generally with lighter weight construction and higher volume capacity than other bulk vans.

cutter head: a device mounted on a mobile machine designed to cut trees at ground level using a hydraulic saw.

delimbing gate: a heavy steel grate with large holes, often over 16 feet in length and 6 feet in height, positioned vertically in the forest, to remove limbs from whole-tree stems.

feller buncher: a rubber-tired or track-mounted machine designed to cut trees and accumulate cut stems into piles. Feller buncher cutting heads can be attached directly to carriers that drive up to a tree to cut it (drive-to-tree), or the cutting head can be attached to a swinging boom and reach to a tree to cut it (swing-to-tree).

forwarder: a machine designed to load cut trees or processed material from the ground and transport it to a landing for further processing or loading into transport vehicles.

grapple: a device designed to grasp a tree or log between two arms and lift or move the piece. Grapples are located at the rear of grapples skidders, where they grab the stems and hold them while the skidder drags them from the woods.

harvester: a rubber-tired or track-mounted machine that performs the functions of the feller buncher and the processor.

knuckleboom: a boom extending from the main chassis of a machine used to support a cutting device or grapples for loading material.

processor: a machine designed to delimb, buck to length, and place stems in piles for loading or segregation into products.

shear: a device mounted on a mobile machine capable of cutting a tree stem at ground level using hydraulic pressure to push blades through the stem.

skidder: a rubber-tired or track-mounted machine designed to transport cut trees or processed material to a landing. Grapple skidders transport material by lifting one end with a grapple and dragging the material behind it.

Chapter 4
Biomass Conversion to Energy and Fuels

Phil Badger and Pratap Pullammanappallil

INTRODUCTION

Previous sections of this document deal with the production and harvesting of wood and associated issues, including the fuel properties of wood. For wood to be used for energy, it must be converted into other energy forms such as heat or electricity. This chapter covers the various types of direct combustion, thermochemical and biological gasification, and fast pyrolysis biofuel technologies for conversion of wood into useful energy forms. Also included is a discussion on industrial process heat, space heating and cooling, and electricity generation end-use applications. The latter includes expanded discussions on combined heat and power (CHP) systems, district heating systems, net metering laws, and pertinent environmental regulations.

BACKGROUND

Biomass can be used directly as a solid fuel or converted into gaseous, liquid, or other solid fuel forms. It can, thus, substitute for or supplement virtually any other energy source and is presently widely used in its raw form as boiler fuel in the paper industry. Liquid fuels are currently of particular interest because of U.S. dependence on imported petroleum, rising petroleum costs, and energy security issues associated with petroleum. Biomass is the only renewable source of liquid fuels that currently exists.

Three things are required for combustion to occur: (1) fuel, (2) oxygen, and (3) a heat source to raise the fuel above its ignition temperature. The rate of burning is usually controlled by limiting the amount of fuel present or, less often, by regulating the amount of combustion air present. However, insufficient combustion air may result in incomplete combustion, which reduces the burner efficiency and can cause air pollution.

As discussed in chapter 3, wood can vary widely in its physical and chemical characteristics. Devices that convert biomass to energy require certain fuel characteristics in order to process them. Furthermore, the energy produced or how it is eventually used is dependent on conversion technology. Fuel preparation must change the characteristics inherent in fuel into characteristics needed for the conversion device in a cost-effective way, while meeting acceptable environmental standards.

Moisture content is an important wood fuel characteristic since the maximum moisture content permissible for wood as a fuel is in the range of 65 to 68 percent.[1] Above this moisture content percentage, the energy required to evaporate the moisture in the wood is greater than the energy in the dry matter of wood, and combustion cannot occur unless heat is supplied from another source. For all systems, excessive fuel moisture can potentially cause corrosion and blockages of the fuel handling system and a reduction in combustion efficiency. Wood contains acids, and with sufficient moisture, can be quite corrosive.

Fuel particle size must be matched to specific burner types (discussed later). Stringy fuels, such as those associated with hardwood bark, can pose special handling problems. The presence of inorganic materials such as soil can increase ash content and change the ash's chemical nature. Pieces of metal and oversized pieces of biomass can also damage equipment.

The chemical composition of ash is important because certain chemicals can lower the melting point of the ash. Melted ash can coat the inside of boiler surfaces (referred to as slagging) and coat heat transfer surfaces (referred to as fouling). Certain potassium and sodium compounds are the primary cause of slagging and fouling. These chemicals, essential for plant growth, are more concentrated in the fastest growing plants or plant parts, such as leaves, twigs, and bark. In general, the stems of older trees have lower concentrations of these chemicals and do not cause problems with slagging and fouling (Baxter and others 1998).

THERMOCHEMICAL CONVERSION OF BIOMASS FUEL

Thermochemical conversion is the process of breaking down biomass into intermediates by using heat and then upgrading it to fuels through a combination of heat and pressure in the presence of catalysts. Several processes and systems are available to implement the conversion, including combustion, gasification, and anaerobic digestion. The processes are described below.

Direct Combustion Processes and Systems

The three systems commonly used for direct combustion of biomass fuels are: (1) pile, (2) suspension, and (3) fluidized bed combustion (FBC). The actual type of burner selected will depend on variables such as amount and final form of energy needed, ease of permitting, and ability to handle a wide variety of fuels, e.g., agricultural materials, cardboard, and wood; variation in the amount of energy required by the end-use application; and cost of the system (Tennessee Valley Authority 1991).

---

[1] Kiln-dried wood used by furniture manufactures will have a moisture content of 5 to 6 percent. Freshly harvested wood typically has a moisture content of 45 to 50 percent and is considered "green" wood. Therefore, a moisture content of 65 percent is unusually high.

Pile combustion system—Pile combustion systems burn wood fuel in a heaped pile supported on a horizontal or inclined grate[2] or in a thin layer spread across a grate that is either traveling or stationary (**fig. 4.1**). Air for combustion is provided under the grate and above the fuel pile. The spreader stokers, fuel-feed, and distribution systems used with "thin-pile" combustion units are generally quite reliable. Any problems that occur can often be traced to uneven fuel distribution across the grate, which results from either oversized fuel particles or high moisture fuel particles that stick together (Tennessee Valley Authority 1991).

Pile burners are noted for their relatively simple design, low capital and operating costs, and ability to burn a fairly wide range of wood particles and moisture contents. The minimum fuel particle size depends on grate opening size, while maximum fuel particle size depends on grate design and size of the entry point into the combustion chamber. In general, large chunks, stringy bark, or sawdust-size particles may be used in these systems.

Underfeed stokers are another version of a pile burner. Underfeed stoker systems push fuel into the combustion chamber from beneath the burning pile. Usually an auger (a rotating, screw-type device) is used to push fuel into the combustion chamber.

Particles must be small enough to flow with the auger, but not too fine, stringy, or green to cause packing and blockage problems. The optimal particle size range is dependent on auger size.

The least complicated and least expensive of the direct combustion systems, the pile burners are generally used for smaller applications. However, when operating, they contain a large amount of burning fuel which prevents them from being shut off or slowed down quickly. Therefore, these burners are not compatible with energy use applications that have highly variable demands for energy over short periods of time.

Suspension combustion system—As their name implies, suspension combustion systems burn their fuel in suspension. Since particles cannot be suspended for very long, due to the force of gravity, they must be relatively small (typically < one-fourth inch) and dry (typically < 15 percent moisture content) so they will burn quickly while still in suspension. (Tennessee Valley Authority 1991).

One type of suspension burner is the cyclonic burner, which is in the form of a horizontal or vertical cylinder. Wood fuel is blown along the curve of the burn chamber and centrifugal force suspends the particles while they are burned (**fig. 4.2**).

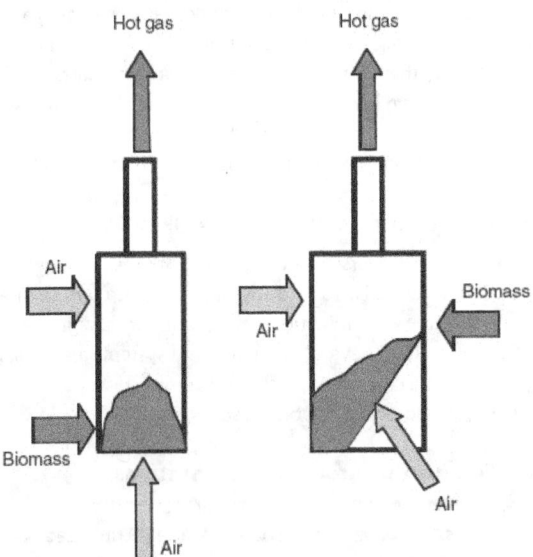

Figure 4.1—Some pile combustion systems burn the wood fuel in a heaped pile supported on either a horizontal or inclined grate.

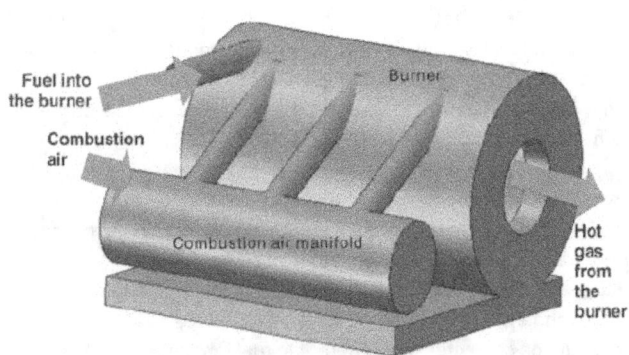

Figure 4.2—Example of a cyclonic burner. Wood is blown into the cylindrical burn chamber so that the small particles of fuel—held by centrifugal force—spiral around the hot walls of the burn chamber while they are burned.

---

[2] A grate may be a flat metal plate to support the fuel while burning with holes in the plate to provide air for combustion. Another type of grate is a wide, moving chain across the bottom of the firebox which carries the fuel through the combustion zone.

Another type of suspension system is the air spreader stoker system, which typically consists of a rectangular firebox with a stationary or traveling grate at the bottom. Wood fuel is horizontally injected with air into the firebox above the grate so that most combustion occurs with the particles in suspension. Unburned particles complete their combustion on the grate. Although suspension burners are limited in their fuel handling capability, these systems are more responsive to changes in heat demands because only a relatively small amount of fuel burns at a given time.

Fluidized bed combustion system—FBC systems burn wood fuel on a high-temperature bed of finely divided chemically inactive (inert) material, such as sand, that is agitated by air blown from beneath the bed. Solid fuel is introduced into the chamber through an airlock, where the fuel particles burn while suspended in the bed (**fig. 4.3**). This suspension allows combustion air to reach all sides of the particles throughout the combustion process, making for highly efficient combustion. The ash produced typically consists of very small particles which are carried from the burner with the hot gases emitted from the burner. The hot gases pass through various devices to capture and control emissions (FBT 1994).

FBC systems are particularly suited to burning a variety of fuels simultaneously, including those that contain high levels of ash, are irregularly shaped, and have high moisture content. Additionally, FBC systems burn the fuel as soon as it is introduced into the burner. This makes FBC systems highly responsive to rapid changes in heat demand. They are also easy to maintain since the combustion chamber does not contain grates that must be cleaned, repaired, and replaced.

On the downside, these systems are relatively complex and have initial costs that are approximately 10 percent higher than grate systems. Also, fuel size is important to effective operation of these systems. Small particles can pass through the unit and may not be caught by the cyclone[3] for recycling back to the bed. Excessively large particles can be too heavy to float in the fluidized bed and may cause problems.

Fuel and bed material are fed into the FBC using under-bed, in-bed, or over-bed feed systems. All of these systems need a pressure seal to force fuel into the FBC and resist backpressure from the bed. A rotary airlock (a paddle wheel turned by a motor to allow particles to pass through it but minimize airflow) is often used for the pressure seal. This type of pressure seal requires fairly uniform particles, and the size of the airlock determines the maximum particle dimensions. The fuel must also be dried so that it will not stick to the conveyors and other parts of the handling system.

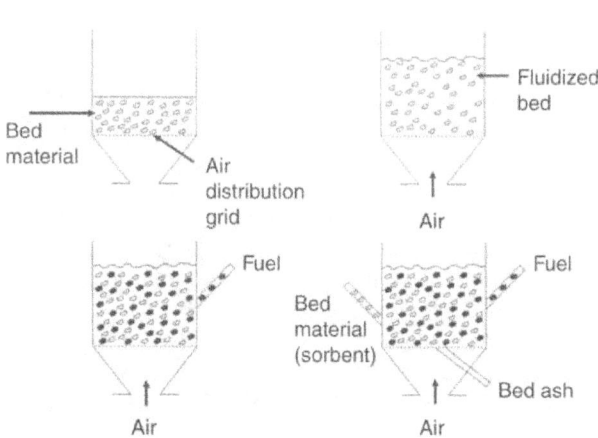

Figure 4.3—Example of a fluidized bed combustion (FBC) unit. In the upper left picture, the system is shut down. In the upper right picture, air is being injected beneath the bed to agitate it. In the lower left picture, fuel is being fed into the bed while the bed is being agitated with air. And in the lower right picture, an absorbent material, such as limestone, is being fed into the bed to absorb sulfur and other pollutants, and ash is shown being removed.

An estimated 2,000 wood-fired, industrial, or commercial wood-energy systems are in use in the Southeastern United States. In general, all of the previously listed types of burners are found in the region. The most common is the grate-type boiler, which generates steam. A distant second place is hot water boilers, followed by hot air systems and thermal fluid (hot oil) heat transfer systems. Grate burner systems are much more common than suspension burner and fluidized bed systems.

Outside of the paper industry, which accounts for an estimated 75 percent of the industrial wood fuel use in the Southeast, most of the wood-fired boilers are used for industrial process heat in the rest of the forest products industry. A small percentage is used by nonforest products industries and commercial entities for process heat (heat used by industries in their manufacturing processes) and heating and cooling. A still slightly smaller percentage is used for heating and cooling schools, prisons, and hospitals, primarily in Georgia and Missouri.

---

[3] A cyclone is a device that uses centrifugal force to remove particles from a rapidly moving airstream. The upper half of the cyclone is a vertical cylinder and the lower half is in the form of a downward pointing cone. The air containing the particles is injected at high speed into the cyclone near the top of the vertical cylinder and along the tangent of the cylinder. The particles in the air are forced out to the cylinder wall by centrifugal force where they slide down into the cone and out the bottom of the cyclone. Clean air exits out of the top center of the cyclone.

Under-bed feed systems usually convey fuel in an airstream within a pipe (pneumatic conveyance), and are more complex than the other types of fuel feed systems. Sizing and drying the fuel are necessary to prevent handling system blockage.

In-bed feed systems are similar to the under-bed feed systems, particularly if fuel is conveyed pneumatically. More complex than over-bed systems, they are generally used for burning high-moisture fuels such as slurries.

Over-bed feed systems include conventional spreader feeders, air swept feeders/mills, and gravity feeders. Less prone to blockages, these systems are simpler to construct and maintain. Since the fuel entry point is above the pressurized bed, there is less pressure on the airlock, reducing the performance requirements of the airlock. For these reasons, over-bed feed systems are most commonly used to feed woody fuels into FBCs.

Gasification Processes

Thermochemical processes, e.g., direct combustion, gasification, and pyrolysis, use heat to cause chemical reactions. If the thermochemical process occurs at high temperature, it is termed a pyrolysis process.

Upon heating, biomass materials decompose into a number of gases and vapors and char. If heated to high enough temperatures in the presence of air, biomass materials will combust. If the biomass is heated in an enclosed container in the absence of air, the gas, vapor, and char cannot burn and can be recovered as products (Klass 1998).

The most common example of a thermochemical process is a direct combustion process, such as a campfire burning wood. The key to understanding the nature of thermochemical processes starts with the direct combustion process. All other thermochemical processes can be thought of as direct combustion processes that have been modified to obtain another desired outcome. The key variables for any thermochemical process are heating rate, final temperature, oxygen levels, pressure, and reaction time. Other important factors include particle size, moisture content, design of the container for the process, biomass chemical composition, and amount and type of ash associated with the material (Georgia Tech 1984).

Decomposition of biomass using thermochemical processes involves a complex reaction system that generates gases, liquids, and solids. Initially, in the direct combustion process, which goes through several distinct stages, heat must be added to biomass material until it reaches its ignition temperature. At that point, it will continue to burn as long as sufficient oxygen is present and the temperature remains at or above the ignition point (Georgia Tech 1984). To summarize, direct combustion consists of the following main steps:
- Drying of biomass material
- Raising the temperature of the material to its ignition point, accompanied by decomposition of the material into gases and vapors
- Further decomposition and evolution of volatiles and gases leaving a char; and
- Combustion of the char, leaving an ash residue

As described in the direct combustion process, gases and vapors are given off at certain points of a thermochemical direct combustion process. One way to thermochemically gasify biomass is to heat it in an enclosed container while allowing a small amount of oxygen to enter. The oxygen allows some combustion to occur, which provides the heat necessary to cause the biomass to decompose into gas, vapor, and char. However, by limiting the amount of oxygen in the container, there is not enough oxygen present to allow the remaining gas and vapor to burn, so these products can be recovered. Because the amount of oxygen is limited, temperature of the gasification process is typically lower than in direct combustion.

The gas and vapor generated can be piped to a boiler or combustion device where it is mixed with oxygen and burned in a manner similar to burning natural gas. The amount of energy in the gas is roughly 150 British thermal units (Btus) per cubic foot. In contrast, natural gas has about 1,000 Btus per cubic foot (Georgia Tech 1984).

Another way to thermochemically gasify biomass is to place it in an enclosed container without any oxygen and heat the container from outside. Since there is no partial combustion, the amount of gas and vapor recovered is higher than with the previously described system. The amount of energy in the gas from these systems can be as high as 500 Btus per cubic foot (FBT 1994).

A similar process can be used to make charcoal. In one charcoal production method, a pile of wood is placed in an enclosed container and ignited. Then the amount of oxygen is restricted so that the wood can only burn slowly. The wood is allowed to smolder for a period of time before all oxygen is cutoff, which eventually causes the fire to go out. The heating process drives most of the gases and vapors out of the wood leaving relatively pure carbon, or charcoal, in its place. A process optimized to produce charcoal would be a slow pyrolysis process and, in comparison to combustion, would operate at relatively low temperatures and take a few hours or days to complete (Georgia Tech 1984).

Most gasifiers are designed so that the biomass is placed inside a container. For these gasifiers to work properly, biomass particles must be large enough for heat to reach them inside the container and provide a path for the gases and vapors to flow out. Another type of gasifier is the fluidized bed gasifier which operates similarly to a fluidized bed combustor (previously described, see fig. 4.3 and accompanying text), except that oxygen is limited inside the container where gasification occurs (FBT 1994).

Biomass gasifiers were widely used to provide fuel for vehicles in Europe and Asia during World War II when petroleum was scarce. These gasifiers were either mounted on the vehicle or on a trailer pulled behind the vehicle (Bridgewater and others 1999).

One way to generate liquid fuels from biomass is through a fast pyrolysis process. A fast pyrolysis process is a gasification process optimized to produce vapor. This is accomplished by rapidly heating the biomass to temperatures between 750 and 1,000 °F within a few seconds and then cooling and condensing the vapors within 2 seconds to recover a liquid. When made from wood, the resulting liquid has an energy content of around 80,000 Btus per gallon, roughly the same as ethanol. The liquid product looks similar to motor oil and is called pyrolysis oil or bio-oil (Bridgewater and others 2002). By performing basically the same process under high pressure (a liquefaction process), the liquid product can have an energy content similar to diesel fuel, about 139,000 Btus per gallon.

Fast pyrolysis processes have several distinct advantages. One is that biomass can be processed into bio-oil at one location and then used at another location in a manner similar to how fuel oil is used. In contrast, a direct combustion or gasification system must be located adjacent to where energy is needed. Thus, biomass must be hauled to the gasifier or direct combustion unit, which is expensive, because biomass is relatively light weight.[4] The gases and, if necessary, the char generated by the fast pyrolysis process can provide thermal energy for the process. These features allow bio-oil to be produced in satellite plants and used in a centralized energy conversion facility; or allow for operation of a central bio-oil production facility in conjunction with distributed energy conversion systems. Thus, bio-oils offer greater flexibility than solid or gaseous fuels (Badger and Fransham 2003).

Anaerobic Digestion

Anaerobic digestion (or biogasification) systems use micro-organisms to break down organic materials under oxygen-free (anaerobic) conditions to produce a biogas. The process occurs in natural environments, and when it is made to occur in engineered environments, it is called anaerobic digestion (digestion since the organic matter is eaten and digested by the micro-organisms).

Anaerobic digestion processes—Anaerobic digestion takes place in two stages as certain micro-organisms feed on organic materials. First, acid-producing bacteria break the complex organic molecules down into simpler sugars, alcohol, glycerol, and peptides. When these substances have accumulated in sufficient quantities, a second group of bacteria convert some of the simpler molecules into methane (Klass 1998).

Like all living things, micro-organisms require environmental conditions that are conducive to their survival and growth. In this case, methane-generating micro-organisms are especially sensitive to environmental conditions. Temperature, acidity (pH), residence time, and amount of water are important environmental conditions for these micro-organisms. For most types of methane digesters, enough water must be present to form a slurry; thus, anaerobic digestions are well suited for treatment of wastewater or slurries high in organic matter. Conversely, anaerobic digestion systems are not well suited for processing dry biomass materials because a large amount of water must be added at the beginning of the process and then discarded at the end of the process (Chynoweth and Jerger 1985).

Anaerobic digestion processes can take hours or days while the microbes grow and reproduce. Therefore, anaerobic digestion processes are slower than thermochemical processes, which can occur in seconds. The biogas typically contains from 50 to 70 percent methane (the main ingredient of natural gas) and has a corresponding energy content of 500 to 700 Btus per cubic foot. The rest of the biogas is typically 30 to 50 percent carbon dioxide, plus small amounts of other gases. Biogas will burn cleanly and can substitute for natural gas in most applications (Chynoweth and others 1991).

There are two main families of micro-organisms in most anaerobic digestion systems. One family likes to have temperatures at 95 to 105 °F and is called a mesophilic system. Another family operates at 125 to 135 °F and is called a thermophilic system. Systems that operate at higher temperatures have the advantage of faster digestion processes. Therefore, the tanks and containers used in these systems can be smaller. However, higher temperature systems have the disadvantage of requiring an outside heat source.

The digestibility of an organic material is measured in terms of the material's volatile solids[5] (VS) content. This material is the part that microbes can literally eat and digest. For this discussion, the focus is on the applicability of anaerobic digestion to woody materials, which are also considered a ligno-cellulosic material. Ligno-cellulose materials are primarily composed of cellulose, hemicellulose, and lignin. The percentage of these constituents depends on the species, age, and growth conditions of the wood. Typically, the relative quantities are 40 to 45 percent cellulose, 20 to 30 percent hemicellulose, and 20 to 30 percent lignin. Even though cellulose and hemicellulose can be anaerobically digested, these materials are relatively difficult to digest since the sugars present must first be broken down. Additionally, lignin encases the cellulose and hemicellulose, making it difficult for microbes to reach them (Jerger and others 1982).

---

[4] Depending on species, a solid block of dry wood will have from 25 to 54 pounds of material in a cubic foot. Chipped green wood has roughly 22 pounds of material in a cubic foot. Dry wood shavings may only have 5 to 6 pounds of material per cubic foot. Thus, trucks hauling biomass may be limited by volume instead of weight. Since wood for energy is usually sold by weight, the relatively low amount of weight that can be transported due to volume limitations can make hauling wood expensive.

[5] Volatile solids (VS): Those solids in water or other liquids that are lost on ignition of the dry solids at 550 °C (http://en.mini.hu/environment/liquid.html).

However, cellulose and hemicellulose components of woody biomass can be converted to methane by anaerobic digestion without pretreatment other than particle size reduction, e.g., grinding (Chynoweth and Jerger 1985, Jerger and others 1982). This is accomplished by utilizing special digester designs that provide good conditions for micro-organisms that work better with woody materials.

Advantages of anaerobic digestion over thermal gasification include:

- Higher moisture content that does not result in reduced efficiency
- Biogas that is a mixture of relatively few gases and that has a higher heating value
- No requirement for oxygen to make medium- or high-energy gas
- A process that can be carried out at ambient pressures and temperatures, and
- An economic process at a variety of scales

Methane yields for various woody biomasses are listed in **table 4.1**. For hardwoods, yields typically range from 3.37 to 6.58 cubic feet of methane per pound of VS. For softwoods like *Eucalyptus* spp. and *Pinus taeda* (loblolly pine), yields range from 0.16 to 0.96 cubic feet of methane per pound of VS (Turick and others 1991).

Anaerobic digester systems—There are several different types of anaerobic digesters. However, only two types, slurry and high-solids (or dry) digesters, will be discussed here because these two types are most suitable for anaerobically digesting

wood. Slurry digesters usually operate with slurries that have over 90 percent water and a few percent solids. High-solids or dry digester designs minimize the use of water. Both designs can be used for woody biomass feedstocks and can be operated in a continuous, semicontinuous, or batch mode. Each digester type has advantages and disadvantages, which change based on the material being digested. Because some digester systems work much better with woody materials than others, not all digester designs will be discussed here.

Slurry digesters stir the slurry inside the digester to keep solid particles mixed in the liquid. These designs are operated at a solids content of 4 to 20 percent, and their benefits include ease of feeding and operation and easy removal of digested effluent. Such designs are commonly used for sewage sludge digestion. For woody biomass, which requires the addition of water to make slurry, this type of design is less efficient than the high-solids type (Chynoweth and Jerger 1982).

Anaerobic digestion with minimal water addition allows digestion of a higher percentage of solids, making smaller digesters as efficient as larger digesters. High-solids or dry anaerobic digesters are typically operated at a solids content of 35 percent. For woody biomass, the performance of dry digesters, like nonmixed vertical flow and two-stage leach-bed packed-bed reactor systems, is superior to slurry digesters. Anaerobic digestion of green waste collected from a municipal solid waste disposal facility produced methane yields of 3.05 and 4.49 cubic feet per pound of VS, respectively, in continuously fed stirred tank anaerobic digesters

Table 4.1—Methane yield of various woody biomass types and comparison to methane yield from cellulose powder

Common name	Scientific name	Methane yield ft^3 per pound of volatile solids
Cellulose powder		6.26
Pussy willow	*Salix eriocephala*	4.66
Shining willow	*S. lucida*	4.33
Coyote willow	*S. exigua*	4.49
Common osier	*S. viminalis*	5.46
White willow	*S. alba*	4.82
Purpleosier willow	*S. purpurea (SP3)*	3.69
Peachleaf willow	*S. amygdaloides (SAM5)*	3.37
Halberd willow	*S. hastata (SH2)*	3.69
Hybrid poplar	*Populus nigra x P. maximowiczii*	6.26
Hybrid poplar	*P. x euramericana*	6.58
Eastern cottonwood	*P. deltoides*	4.82
American sycamore	*Platanus occidentalis*	6.10
Black locust	*Robinia pseudoacacia*	4.82
Sweetgum	*Liquidambar styraciflua*	4.17

Source: Turick and others (1991).

and nonmixed vertical flow reactors operated at a loading rate of 0.1 pound VS per cubic foot per day at mesophilic (100 °F) temperatures (Chynoweth and others 1991). For the same biomass feedstock, at the same loading rate and temperature, a leach-bed packed-bed system produced a methane yield of 5.14 cubic feet per pound of VS.

A schematic diagram of an unmixed vertical flow digester is shown in **figure 4.4**. This process can be operated continuously or semicontinuously. It is a plug flow design wherein the biomass flows from the top of the reactor, where it is fed, to the bottom, without undergoing any mixing. Biomass is digested as it moves down, releasing biogas bubbles that rise to the top. The undigested residue is removed from the bottom of the reactor, and part of it is recycled and mixed back with the feed. The rest is dewatered and disposed of. Leachate[6] from water removal operations is also recycled and mixed with incoming biomass. Mixing undigested residue and leachate with the new material entering the digester provides the new material with micro-

organisms for digestion, nutrients for microbial growth, and optimal moisture for the microbes, while also helping to keep the slurry from becoming too acidic (Chynoweth and others 1991).

A leach-bed packed-bed configuration is shown in **figure 4.5**. This is a batch process and requires two reactors, one containing a bed of fresh biomass that is to be digested and the other containing anaerobically digested residue. Water is added to the feedstock (reactor 1) in excess of saturation capacity to moisten it and produce leachate that collects at the bottom of the bed. This leachate is flushed through the stabilized residue (reactor 2) and leachate from the stabilized residue (reactor 2) is flushed to the top of the fresh bed of biomass (reactor 1).

This leachate exchange strategy provides numerous benefits to initiation of anaerobic digestion in the fresh biomass. Initially, fermentation reactions that produce volatile organic acids are started in the bed of fresh biomass. Water flushed through the bed leaches out these organic acids, which are then flushed through

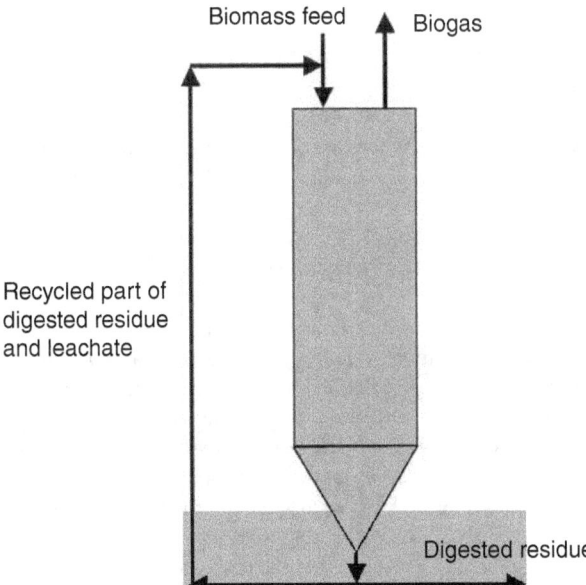

Figure 4.4—A schematic diagram of an unmixed vertical flow digester. In operation, wet biomass continuously flows into the top of the digester and slowly settles to the bottom while microbes digest the biomass. The biogas bubbles to the top of the digester where the gas is collected and piped to where it can be used. Undigested residue is removed from the bottom of the digester and part of the residue is recycled back to the top of the digester to seed the incoming biomass with microbes.

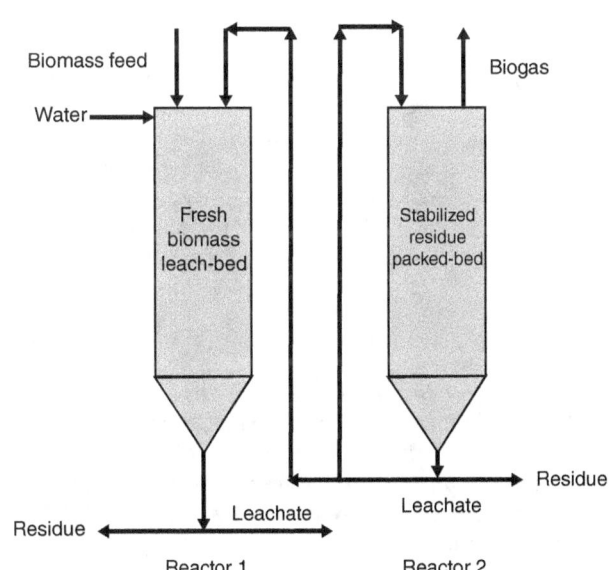

Figure 4.5—A leach-bed packed-bed biogasification system. In operation, biomass is placed into the digester in a batch. The second container contains mostly water and some previously digested biomass. A water/biomass mixture from the second digester is slowly circulated through the bed of fresh biomass in the first reactor to seed the biomass with microbes and cause digestion to occur. The resulting biogas product bubbles to the top of the digester where the gas is collected and piped to its end-use point. After biogas production stops, the spent residue is removed from the digester and the process repeated with a new batch.

---

[6] A leachate is a liquid that collects at the bottom of the reactor. It can usually contain both dissolved and suspended material.

the stabilized residue. The stabilized residue, having already undergone anaerobic digestion, contains the methane-generating microbes that consume the volatile organic acids from the fresh bed of biomass. Some of these methane-generating microbial populations are also flushed out with the leachate, which serves to inoculate the bed of fresh biomass. In addition to providing seed microbes, this leachate exchange strategy provides nutrients and a pH buffer to the fresh biomass to help sustain the microbial populations. Once this reseeding has been initiated in the fresh bed, leachate is only recirculated to keep the bed moist. The spent and now stabilized residue can either be disposed of or used to initiate methane generation in another batch of biomass (Chynoweth and others 1991).

WOODY BIOMASS END USES AND POWER GENERATION

For the solar energy stored in wood to be of practical use, it must be converted into a more useful form of energy. The near-term uses of wood for energy include industrial process heat, heating and cooling buildings, and electrical power generation. Most wood is burned, but some is converted to gas and burned to produce steam, hot water, hot air, or hot oil that can be used to carry and distribute the heat to other locations.

Boilers, to generate steam or hot water, consist of an enclosed tank with tubes that pass through one wall of the tank and out another side of the tank. In firetube boilers, the hot air and gases from combustion (stack gases) pass through the tubes of the boiler, and the water is contained in the surrounding tank. Watertube boilers are the opposite, with water flowing through the tubes and the hot stack gases on the outside of the tubes. Firetube boilers are less expensive to make and can be used in low-pressure

A common mistake made by engineers unfamiliar with wood-fired systems is to design the system so that it is normally operating in the middle instead of the upper end of its operating range. Unlike most fossil fuel-fired systems, the efficiency of wood-fired systems typically falls off rapidly below the upper end of its operating range. Fossil-fueled systems are frequently oversized to make sure that they meet their performance requirements; however, their efficiency stays relatively constant in the upper end of their operating range so that their system efficiency is not significantly hurt.

steam applications. Watertube boilers are more expensive to manufacture because they use many small-diameter tubes, which are required for higher steam pressures (Georgia Tech 1984).

Because boilers generate steam at relatively high pressure,[7] their use is closely regulated, and they are more costly to construct and operate than other systems. Hot water systems do not carry as much energy per pound of water as steam systems; therefore, larger amounts of heat transfer surfaces are required when using hot water systems. However, hot water systems are less expensive to build and operate than steam systems because they can operate with little or no pressure. Hot air systems are only used when the heat does not have to be transferred very far, such as in heating a commercial or residential building or lumber dry kiln (Georgia Tech 1984).

Hot oil systems combine the best aspects of steam and hot water systems and are competitive with steam systems in capital cost and less expensive to operate. Some hot oils (also called heat transfer fluids) can be heated to over 600 °F without pressurizing the system. Thus, hot oil systems can reach the temperatures that steam systems reach without using elevated pressures. Oil systems do not require a boiler operating license or water treatment system (since they do not use water), and they do not create freezeup problems.[8]

Industrial processes use heat in a variety of ways, including paint drying, cooking, sterilizing, pasteurizing food, setting dyes in cloth, and melting metals. Using energy to heat and cool buildings (also called space heating and cooling) is similar to using it for industrial processes, except that, in the case of energy use for a building, energy is transferred to a heat exchanger in the building being heated.

Cooling With Wood

Energy from wood can also be used to cool buildings. One method is to use wood to generate electricity that powers a conventional electrically powered air conditioning system (compression cycle). Another method is to replace the electric motor on the air conditioner's compressor with a steam turbine. A more common method is to use low-pressure steam to activate absorption chillers. Early refrigerators in the United States operated on natural gas to provide a source of heat that activated an absorption system. Absorption systems were later replaced by the more efficient compression cycle systems that still are commonly part of the modern refrigerator. However, the absorption system has the major advantage of using low-temperature waste heat, including low-pressure steam. Absorption systems are still widely used in the United States in CHP applications (Wiltsee 1994, Guinn 1992).

---

[7] Utility boilers typically operate at high-steam pressures and high-steam temperatures. Steam with a gauge pressure of 2,000 pounds per square inch will have a temperature of 1,000 ºF.

[8] Personal communication. 2006. David Gamble. President. Green Energy Technologies, P.O. Box 159, Moody, AL 35133.

Although many people have tried to develop cost-effective wood-fired cooling systems for residential and commercial applications, the development of such systems has not been successful. Usually, industrial wood-fueled cooling systems can be cost effective only if large quantities of waste heat are available at temperatures sufficient to operate absorption chillers. Nevertheless, industrial chillers based on absorption systems are more commonly used today than most people realize (Wiltsee 1994). For a good example of an industrial success story, see text box below for a discussion of the CHP heating and cooling system used in La-Z-Boy® Furniture manufacturing plants (SERBEP 1997). [9]

District Heating Systems

District heating systems use one or more central plants, e.g., a boiler, and distribute heat via pipes to two or more buildings to supply space heat or hot water for domestic use. Sometimes district heating systems are used to provide process heat to industrial users either in combination with residential, commercial, or institutional users, or with a district heating system to serve a specific industrial park.

Central systems reduce capital and operating costs because they reduce the number of plants and the number of crews required for staffing the plants, and they are more efficient than smaller plants. Capital costs are reduced even though additional piping is required between the plant and the various buildings where heat is used. Air quality is improved since it is easier and more cost effective to put pollution control equipment on a central plant than on many small dispersed plants (Maker and Penny 1999).

District heating systems are frequently used on college campuses and State institutions where several buildings are close together and under the control of one authority. In northern climates, district heating systems frequently serve entire towns, apartment complexes, villages, or parts of large cities. For example, large wood-fired district heating systems commonly serve entire communities in Scandinavia. In 1999, Finland and Denmark supplied 50 percent of their respective space heating needs with district heating systems, while Sweden provided 3 percent (Maker and Penny 1999).

District heating systems offer several advantages for both the customer and the community. Customers do not have to own and operate their own heating systems or procure and store fuel onsite. The central plants are operated around the clock by trained professionals, and the systems have backup boilers and standby power generators in case of power outages. For these and other reasons, district heating systems historically have had a high level of reliability.

La-Z-Boy® Furniture Company, a major manufacturer of upholstered furniture, uses wood waste-fueled CHP systems in all of its furniture manufacturing plants. The company purchases green lumber from sawmills, and kiln dries the wood onsite. The wood, roughly 90 percent soft maple (Acer spp.), is processed for frame components, and all the sawdust and wood scraps are conveyed pneumatically to silos for storage. This approach has been in place since the company's first wood-fired boiler was installed in 1974 at its Dayton, TN, facility.

The original boiler system has been upgraded to improve controls and efficiencies, and to increase capacities due to plant expansions. The current system now consists of a wood-fired boiler system [30,000 lbm steam at 300 psi] and two 350-kW backpressure turbines. Heat is used for dry kilns, for heating 900,000 square feet of floor space, for air conditioning, and for generating electricity. When building heat is required, steam from the backpressure turbines heats water that circulates through the plant to unit heaters. If cooling is required, the steam from the backpressure turbines is sent to an absorption chiller, which chills water in the same circulation loop used for heating. When mornings are chilly and afternoons hot in the spring and fall, the same system is used for heating in the morning and cooling in the afternoon. The CHP system saves the company on electricity costs, eliminates landfilling of 10,000 tons per year of wood waste, and improves working conditions for plant employees.

Since 1983, downtown St. Paul, MN, has been served by a hot water district heating system that originally burned coal, oil, and natural gas. In 2001, on the same site, District Energy of St. Paul opened a companion wood-fired CHP system equipped with a 25-MWe backpressure turbine. The plant uses 275,000 tons per year of municipal tree trimmings and clean wood wastes, and provides heating, cooling, and electricity to 141 large buildings and 298 single-family residences through 15 miles of pipe. The system heats over 23 million square feet of floor space, or about 75 percent of the city's downtown area.

---

[9] Additional information on cooling with wood is available in "Heat-Activated Cooling Devices: A Guidebook for General Audiences" and "Design Guide for Thermally Activated Air Conditioning". The publications are available from General* Bioenergy at www.bioenergyupdate.com.

District heating systems that are constructed to be fuel-flexible can provide more stable heating costs than those strictly using fossil fuels. This is especially true of systems designed to use biomass fuels. Frequently, district heating systems can obtain low-cost waste heat from industrial processes or utility plants. Many communities view the relatively inexpensive energy that comes from district heating systems as an incentive to draw new businesses. Some communities even have set up entire industrial parks around district energy systems (Maker and Penny 1999).

Electric Power Production

Typically, electricity-generating plants generate steam with boilers, from which power is generated by passing the steam through steam turbines, as shown in **figure 4.6**. This process is also known as a Rankine cycle. The amount of electricity generated is directly proportional to the flow rate of steam and the drop in steam pressure as the steam flows through the turbine and releases its energy. Thus, to maximize power production, the pressure drop must be maximized.

The efficiency of steam turbines is low for very small turbines. Larger turbines are more efficient, partly because they can use multistage turbines that pass the steam sequentially through several sets of turbine blades to maximize energy extraction (Wiltsee 1993).

Under the best scenario, only about one-third of the energy in the fuel that goes into the boiler comes out as electrical energy. The rest of the energy is in the form of low-temperature steam, hot water, or hot air. Although the quantities of waste heat generated by a power plant may be quite large, the usefulness of this heat is limited by its low temperature. This is because the transfer of heat requires a temperature difference, with larger temperature differences providing more efficient heat transfer. Waste heat discharged from coal-fired power plants is typically in the range of 70 to 90 °F, which limits the applications for which the heat may be used (Hubert and Madewell 1987).

CHP or cogeneration plants recover some of the heat from power generation for useful purposes. One way heat is recovered is with a backpressure turbine. Backpressure turbines do not have a condenser on their steam exit but instead regulate steam flow

A s a rule of thumb, 1 dry ton per hour or 2 green tons per hour of wood fuel can generate 1 MW of electricity. In the strictest sense, a dry ton of wood contains no moisture. However, in practice, a dry ton of wood frequently refers to wood that has a moisture content of 10 percent or less. A green ton of wood contains > 10 percent water and usually refers to wood containing 40 to 50 percent water, a moisture content typical for wood freshly harvested in the summer.

I n general, at least 100-psig steam pressure is required for steam flow sufficient to operate a steam turbine. Some turbines may require even higher pressures. It is a common mistake to install a steam boiler with the intention of generating electricity in the future and later discovering that the boiler does not have sufficient pressure for power generation.

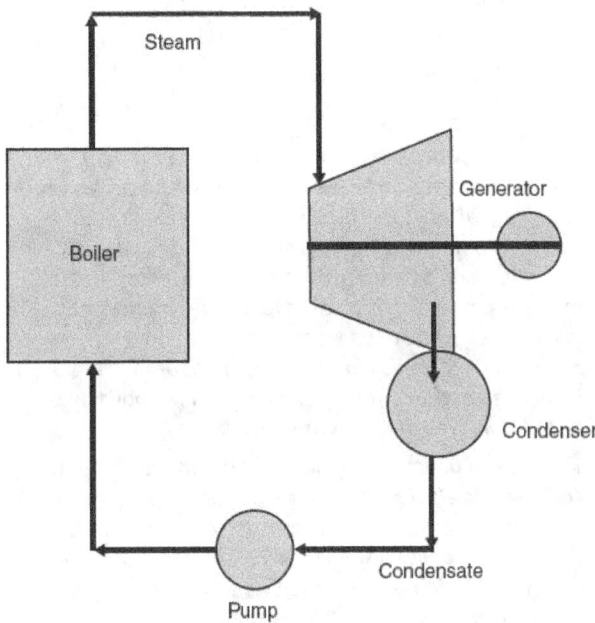

Figure 4.6—A diagram of a condensing steam turbine system. Steam from the boiler is passed through a steam turbine which powers a generator to generate electricity. A condenser on the steam outlet port of the turbine condenses any remaining steam back into a liquid so that it can be pumped back into the boiler to repeat the cycle. Since 4,000 cubic inches of steam will condense into one cubic inch of water, condensing the spent steam also creates a vacuum at the port of the turbine. And since the efficiency of the turbine depends on the flow rate of steam and the pressure drop of the steam as it flows through the turbine, the act of condensing the steam also increases the efficiency of the electricity generation process. However, the act of condensing the steam requires dumping a large amount of heat in the form of hot air or hot water. This water or air is usually at such a low temperature that it has little or no value and consequently, the energy is lost. A large amount of energy is required to inject spent steam from the turbine—which is at a relatively low pressure when it exits the turbine—back into the boiler. Therefore, in order to maximize electrical production, the steam is condensed into a liquid which can be much more cost effectively injected back into the boiler. In addition, condensing the steam creates a vacuum, which further increases the pressure drop across the turbine and increases generating efficiency.

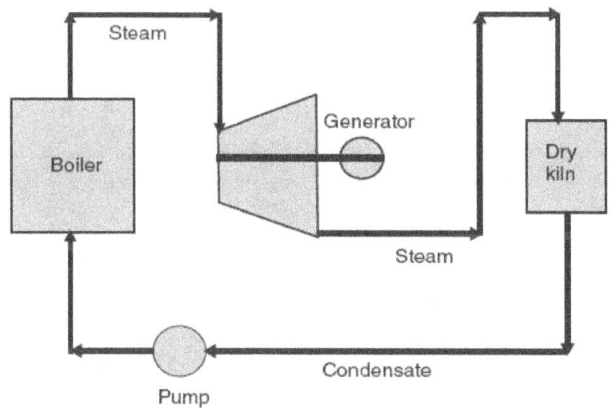

Figure 4.7—A diagram of a backpressure (noncondensing) steam turbine system. Steam from the boiler is passed through a steam turbine which powers a generator to generate electricity. However, the system is designed so that the steam exiting the turbine still has some pressure left (typically 15 psi). The low pressure provides the energy to move the steam through a pipeline to a point where the steam can be used and, in the process, condensed back to a liquid. Forest product industries frequently will use these systems to generate electricity and heat dry kilns to dry lumber. Since the efficiency of the turbine depends on the flow rate of steam and the pressure drop of the steam as it flows through the turbine, the decrease in pressure drop across the turbine also decreases the efficiency of the electricity generation process. However, more of the overall energy is recovered from this type of process, so that the backpressure turbine is more cost effective.

to provide low-pressure steam, e.g., 15 pounds per square inch, from the turbine (**fig. 4.7**) (Guinn 1990). Steam at level pressure has enough energy to be useful and also enough pressure to move the steam to its intended point of use. However, the amount of electricity that can be generated is reduced because the pressure drop across the turbine has been decreased. Although the amount of electricity production has decreased, the overall system efficiency has increased due to the capture and use of heat that was formerly wasted. This concept is illustrated in **figure 4.8**.

Another way to recover useful steam from a steam turbine is through an extraction turbine (**fig. 4.9**). An extraction turbine operates like a condensing turbine except that steam is extracted at a point as it flows across the turbine instead of being recovered as it exits the turbine. The point of extraction depends on how much steam pressure is required. Extraction turbines can be designed to match the steam flow and pressures required for a specific application, thus, better matching steam flow to heat demand for the end-use application. It is not possible to maximize both heat and electricity generation—one is always at the expense of the other. As a rule, it is best to maximize the most valuable energy in a CHP system, which is usually electricity (Guinn 1990).

CHP applications work best when there is a year-round steady demand for both electricity and heat. Certain industries, e.g.,

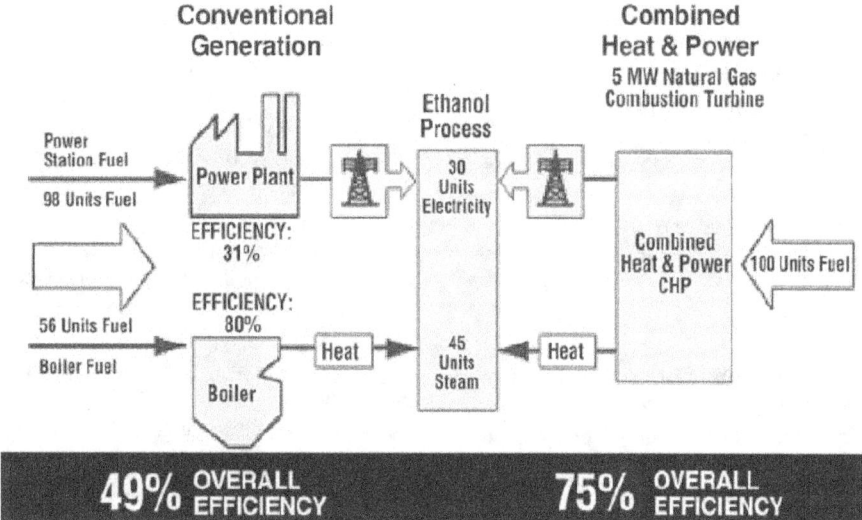

Figure 4.8—An example of a CHP system for an ethanol plant. In this example the industrial facility needs 30 units of electricity and 45 units of steam. The facility can purchase the electricity from the local power company, where the power company uses 98 units of fuel to generate 30 units of electricity at 31 percent efficiency. The company could also install a boiler (or purchase steam from another source) to provide 45 units of steam, which requires 56 units of fuel at 80 percent efficiency. Alternatively, the company could install a CHP system at the facility which would provide the same 30 units of electricity and 45 units of steam. The CHP system would only require 100 units of fuel (versus the 154 units required by separate sources of steam and electricity) and would have an overall system efficiency of 75 percent. In addition, the self-generation of power can provide less variation in the voltage fluctuations over grid supplied power and, depending on how the system is designed, a means of standby power.

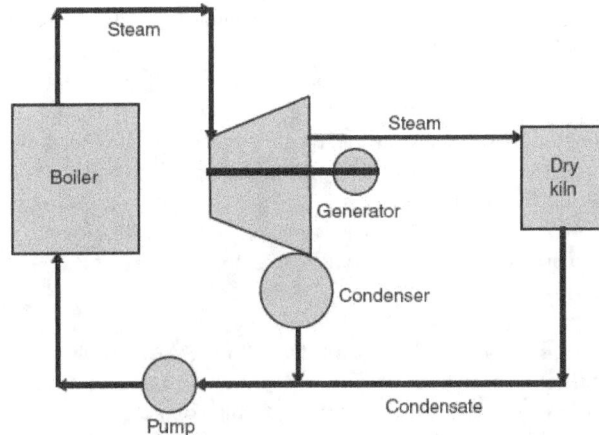

Figure 4.9—A diagram of an extraction steam turbine system. In principle and as shown in the diagram, the extraction system is a hybrid of the condensing and backpressure systems. As steam flows through the turbine, it will drop in pressure. Therefore, by addition of a port at the appropriate place on the turbine casing, steam can be extracted at a desired pressure and quantity. Thus, steam can be extracted and used for an industrial process or other application that requires more steam pressure and flow than can be provided with a backpressure turbine.

forest operations that require kilns for drying lumber, and certain institutions, e.g., hospitals, prisons, and colleges, are particularly good candidates for CHP systems.

Determining a cost-effective, minimum-size, wood-fired, steam-turbine, electricity-generating system is not easy, as it depends on several factors. However, in certain conditions, wood-fired boilers around 600 boiler horsepower and that generate 300 to 1000 kW of electricity in CHP applications may be cost effective (Easterly and Lowenstein 1986). Typically, to be cost effective, the boilers must produce electricity that is valued at retail electricity purchases, and that generates significant revenue from its thermal energy. If one were also paying to get rid of wood residues, the inhouse use of these residues for electricity generation would improve the cost effectiveness of CHP systems (Wiltsee 1993).

Types of generators—There are two basic types of electricity generators: the induction generator and synchronous generator. Generators require a magnetic field to generate electricity. An induction generator uses electricity from the grid to create the magnetic field of the generator. Therefore, an induction generator cannot operate if it cannot receive electricity from the utility grid. Induction generators are, therefore, useless for standby power generation. Their significant advantages are low cost, simplicity, and reliability.

Synchronous generators are more complex because they are designed to operate on or off the grid. However, they require

complex controls to match their electrical output to that of the grid. Synchronous generators are, thus, more costly to install and operate. Utility power plants use synchronous generators exclusively (Guinn 1990).

Independent power plants—Independent power plants are electricity-generating plants that operate outside of a regulated utility business structure and sell power to a utility. The 45-MW wood-fired plant at New Bern, NC, and the 45-MW wood, landfill-gas, and tire-crumb plant in Lakeland, FL, are two examples. Typically, these plants use stoker-fired steam boilers and turbines.

Cofiring—Some boilers can burn wood fuel in a process called cofiring that burns wood and coal simultaneously in the same boiler. As discussed previously, types of burners for wood vary according to the form of fuel, the size of installation, and other factors. Boilers that use spreader stokers can cofire wood and coal together on a grate, providing that the wood and coal particles are large enough not to fall through the grate. Because of the difference in bulk density and other characteristics governing the handling of each fuel, wood and coal are typically stored and fed separately to the spreader stoker. The main boiler on the campus of the University of Missouri is an example of such a system (Foster Wheeler 1997).

Large utility plants typically pulverize coal to a talcum powder consistency and then burn it in suspension. The use of small particles and complete exposure of the particles to air allows the particles to burn quickly and efficiently, as required for suspension burn systems (Foster Wheeler 1997).

There are two methods of feeding wood fuels into coal plants for purposes of cofiring, each with its advantages and disadvantages. One method is to process the wood through the coal handling equipment and feed wood and coal together (commingled) into the plant. While the easiest and lowest cost method, it also has the disadvantage of limitations on the amount of wood that can be used (typically, no more than 7 percent of the boiler's gross energy input but for some boilers, no more than 4 percent) (Foster Wheeler 1997). This limitation stems from the small wood-handling capacity of pulverizers (wood is fibrous and difficult to pulverize), as well as from difficulties inherent in conveying the mixture of wood and coal into the boiler (wood and coal particles conveyed pneumatically tend to separate at higher levels of wood content). The cost of equipping a plant to cofire commingled wood and coal ranges from $100 to $250/kW.[10]

Another method of cofiring is to process and feed wood and coal separately and feed each fuel into the boiler separately. The method uses a separate pulverizer especially designed for wood fuels and blows the pulverized wood, separately from the coal, into the boiler. A distinct advantage of this method is a greater

---

[10] Personal communication. 2006. Evan Hughes. Consultant. 30 Rondo Way, Menlo Park, CA 94025.

capacity for handling wood, up to 10 to 20 percent more than the commingled method. Disadvantages include the possible problems of boiler derating or slagging and fouling at higher levels. Boiler derating occurs because the energy in wood (8,500 Btus per dry pound) is less than in coal (12,000 Btus per dry pound). Thus, if each pound of coal is replaced with a pound of wood, less electricity will be produced. Another disadvantage is the expense of feeding of fuels separately, with the cost of converting a plant to this method ranging from $200 to $300/kW or, if drying of the wood is required, up to $500/kW (see footnote 11).

Another option for using wood at existing coal plants is to install a wood gasifier adjacent to the coal plant and feed gas from the gasifier into the coal boiler's firebox. Gasification occurs at lower temperatures, mitigating slagging and fouling problems.[11]

A third option that is rapidly becoming available is to use a wood distillate product called bio-oil or pyrolysis oil, made by fast pyrolysis processes. With this option, small satellite plants located close to the biomass convert wood into distillate. The wood distillate, a liquid with considerably more energy per cubic foot than the wood, is then trucked to the plant. The higher energy density of the distillate translates into cheaper and simpler handling and operations. Fewer trucks are needed for transporting the fuel; and handling at the utility plant is streamlined because the need for truck scales, truck dumpers, wood storage, and other associated equipment has been eliminated. Instead, a typical fuel oil handling system consists of a fuel tank and pump for transferring the liquid into the boiler. Usually, existing ports in the boiler can be used to inject the distillate into the boiler. The alkali metals in the wood remain in the ash and char produced during the wood distillation process and, thus, are not an issue with the boiler (Badger and Fransham 2003).

A process called reburning makes further use of wood in utility burners. Fuel, the wood distillate, is injected into the stack gas just above the main burner in the boiler where it burns under conditions of limited oxygen. The reburning converts the harmful nitrogen oxides in the emissions into elemental nitrogen, which is not harmful and is plentiful in our atmosphere (Brouwer and others 1997).

Selling Electricity to Others

The best way for an industry to maximize profits from power production is by using its power inhouse. Known as "behind the meter," this use of power occurs on the customer side of the electric meter. Inhouse use directly offsets retail purchases of electricity and, thus, maximizes profitability.

Another option for maximizing profit is to sell power back to the utility company, although such sales are usually not cost effective due to the low cost of utility-generated power. Some States have net metering laws that require utilities to purchase power at the same rate that they sell it to the customer. Most net metering requirements limit the amount of electricity that the utility must purchase to relatively small amounts, e.g., 100 kW, and also restrict the types of generation processes.

A third option is to sell electricity to a customer other than a utility company. However, most State regulatory bodies classify a utility as any entity that sells electricity to more than one customer, and such classification adds to an operation a significant level of regulation and associated expense. It may be possible to avoid regulatory restrictions by bringing in electric customers as project partners or offering alternate arrangements, e.g., selling the customer steam and letting the customer generate his or her own power (Wiltsee 1993).

Permits and Regulations Related to Siting

The permits and regulations that apply to locating and installing a biomass conversion or processing facility cover land use, environmental concerns, and health and safety issues. States are responsible for enforcing environmental regulations established by the U.S. Environmental Protection Agency, but because States also can establish more stringent guidelines, wide variation in regulations may exist from State to State (U.S. Environmental Protection Agency 2006).

Environmental regulations may cover air emissions from any source, including those that produce dust, as well as water quality related to wastewater emissions or runoff from biomass storage systems. Solid waste regulations may apply if wood is considered a waste or contains nonwood material, such as preservatives, fire retardants, or paints. Federal wetlands regulations may also apply.

The primary permitting requirements usually pertain to air emissions, with particulates typically the emission of concern. Fortunately, particulate emissions are relatively easy to control with simple mechanical devices such as cyclones and baghouses.

Land use regulations may include local zoning laws, building codes, permits to store combustible liquids onsite, and access to public roads (rights-of-way). If the proposed site is not already zoned for industrial, a variance or special permit will be required. Building codes may require approvals from the local fire department as well as electrical, mechanical, and plumbing inspections.

---

[11] Personal communication. 2006. Thomas W. Johnson. Head. Research & Environmental Affairs Department, Southern Company Services Inc., 600 North 18th St., Birmingham, AL 335226.

Health and safety regulations include boiler permits and inspections as well as Federal Occupational Safety and Health Administration (OSHA) requirements. OSHA regulations require the presence of two people onsite when machinery is operating, although the second person can be employed in work independent of plant operations.

The cost and time of obtaining permits and meeting regulatory codes can be significant. Local environmental firms familiar with State and local codes and procedures can help make sure all regulations are met and necessary procedures followed. No physical site preparation can be conducted until all permits are in place. Therefore, the permitting process should be given the utmost attention and adequate resources should be committed to its completion.

CONCLUSIONS

Wood can be converted into fuel in solid, liquid, and gaseous forms and can supplement or replace any other energy source. Various types of wood-burning devices are commercially available and are built to handle specific requirements based on what form the wood is in, e.g., chips, sticks, or sawdust; the size of the burner required; and the form of energy needed, e.g., process heat or electricity.

End-use options for wood energy include industrial process heat, space heating and cooling, and electricity generation. CHP systems efficiently generate power and use the leftover heat for industrial or commercial applications. District heating systems, whether used with CHP or as stand-alone heat sources, can create an economy of scale through centralized heat sources serving many customers in a concentrated geographical area. The most cost-effective industrial scenarios involve use of CHP systems and inhouse consumption of all onsite-generated electricity.

The use of wood energy systems is likely to grow because the systems are easy to use, relatively cost effective, widely available, and supported by an existing production and supply infrastructure.

REFERENCES

Badger, Phillip C.; Fransham, Peter. 2003. Use of mobile fast pyrolysis plants to densify biomass and reduce biomass handling costs—a preliminary assessment. Biomass and Bioenergy. 30(4): 321–325.

Baxter, Larry L.; Miles, Thomas R.; Miles, Thomas R., Jr. [and others]. 1998. The behavior of inorganic material in biomass-fired power boilers: field and laboratory experiences. Fuel Processing Technology. 54: 47-78.

Bridgewater, A.; Czernik, Diebold, J.; Meier, D. Oasmaaa [and others]. 1999. Energy from biomass-a review of combustion and gasification technologies. World Bank Tech. Pap. 422. Washington, DC: World Bank. 78 p.

Bridgewater, A.V.; Czernik, S.; Piskorz, J. 2002. The status of biomass fast pyrolysis. In: Bridgwater, A.V., ed. Fast Pyrolysis of Biomass: A handbook. Newbury, UK: CPL Press: 1-22. Vol. 2.

Brouwer, J.; Harding, N.S.; Heap, M.P. [and others]. 1997. An evaluation of wood reburning for NOx reduction from stationary sources. . Publ. TV–92271. Muscle Shoals, AL: U.S. Department of Energy, Southeastern Regional Biomass Energy Program; Tennessee Valley Authority. 59 p. https:// www.bioenergyupdate.com. [Date accessed: January 27, 2010].

Chynoweth, David P.; Bosch, G.; Earle, J.F.K. [and others]. 1991. A novel process for anaerobic composting of municipal solid waste. Applied Biochemistry and Biotechnology. 28/29: 421–432.

Chynoweth, David P.; Jerger, Douglas E. 1985. Anaerobic digestion of woody biomass. Developments in industrial microbiology. Society for Industrial Microbiology. 26: 235–246.

Easterly, James L.; Lowenstein, Michael Z. 1986. Cogeneration from biofuels: a technical guidebook. Publ. TV–67207A. Muscle Shoals, AL: U.S. Department of Energy, Southeastern Regional Biomass Energy Program; Tennessee Valley Authority. 118 p.

FBT, Inc. 1994. Fluidized bed combustion and gasification: a guide for biomass waste generators. Publ. TV-91323. Muscle Shoals, AL: U.S. Department of Energy, Southeastern Regional Biomass Energy Program; Tennessee Valley Authority. 228 p. (available at www.bioenergyupdate.com)

Foster Wheeler Environmental Corporation. 1997. Biomass cofiring guidelines. EPRI TR–108952. Palo Alto, CA: Electric Power Research Institute. 71 p.

Georgia Tech (Georgia Institute of Technology). 1984. The industrial wood energy handbook. New York: Van Nostrand Reinhold Co. 240 p.

Guinn, Gerald R. 1990. Design manual for small steam turbines. Publ. TV–76680. Muscle Shoals, AL: U.S. Department of Energy, Southeastern Regional Biomass Energy Program; Tennessee Valley Authority. 104 p. https://www.bioenergyupdated.com. [Date accessed: January 27, 2010].

Guinn, Gerald R. 1992. Design guide for thermally activated air conditioning. Publ. TV–84063. Muscle Shoals, AL: U.S. Department of Energy, Southeastern Regional Biomass Energy Program; Tennessee Valley Authority. 94 p. https://www.bioenergyupdate.com. [Date accessed: January 27, 2010].

Hubert, Wayne A.; Madewell, Carl E. 1978. State of the art waste heat utilization for agriculture and aquaculture. Bull. Y–132. Muscle Shoals, AL: Tennessee Valley Authority; Electric Power Research Institute; TVA National Fertilizer Development Center. 360 p.

Jerger, Douglas E.; Dolenc, Dan A.; Chynoweth, David P. 1982. Bioconversion of woody biomass as a renewable source of energy. Biotechnology and Bioengineering Symposium. 12: 233–248.

Klass, D.L. 1998. Biomass for renewable energy, fuels, and chemicals. San Diego, CA: Academic Press. 651 p.

Maker, Timothy; Penny, Janet. 1999. Heating communities with renewable fuels: the municipal guide to biomass district heating. Essex Junction, VT: Community Renewable Energy. 52 p. (available at www.bioenergyupdate.com)

SERBEP. 1997. Tennessee biomass—La-Z-Boy of Tennessee [Fact sheet]. Muscle Shoals, AL: Tennessee Valley Authority. Prepared for the TVA/DOE Southeastern Regional Biomass Energy Program. 2 p.

Tennessee Valley Authority. 1991. Biomass design manual: industrial size systems. Muscle Shoals, AL: U.S. Department of Energy, Southeastern Regional Biomass Program. 176 p. (available at www.bioenergyupdate.com)

Turick, C.E.; Peck, M.W.; Chynoweth, D.P. [and others]. 1991. Methane fermentation of woody biomass. Bioresource Technology. 37: 141–147.

U.S. Environmental Protection Agency, Combined Heat and Power Partnership. 2006. Combined heat and power – an energy efficient choice for the ethanol industry. www.epa.gov/chp. [Date accessed: June 21, 2006].

Wiltsee, G. 1993. Small-scale biomass fueled cogeneration systems—a guidebook for general audiences. Publ. TV–89669-2. Muscle Shoals, AL: U.S. Department of Energy, Southeastern Regional Biomass Energy Program; Tennessee Valley Authority. 31 p. (available at www.bioenergyupdated.com)

Wiltsee, G. 1994. Heat activated cooling devices: a guidebook for general audiences. Publ. TV–89669-1. Muscle Shoals, AL: U.S. Department of Energy, Southeastern Regional Biomass Energy Program; Tennessee Valley Authority. 25 p. (available at www.bioenergyupdated.com)

Glossary of Terms

absorption cooling system: a type of cooling system that causes cooling by absorbing a gaseous refrigerant in a fluid and then, in a separate operation, heating the fluid to release the energy in the refrigerant.

alkali metal salts: primarily potassium and sodium metals in wood ash in the form of oxides, hydroxides, and metallo-organic compounds that may cause slagging and fouling when the wood is combusted.

anaerobic digestion (also called biogasification): processes that use micro-organisms to break down organic materials under oxygen-free (anaerobic) conditions to produce a biogas. The process occurs in natural environments, and when it is made to occur in engineered environments, it is called anaerobic digestion (digestion since the organic matter is eaten and digested by the micro-organisms).

anaerobic digester: a system of tanks and other equipment that employs an anaerobic digestion process to break down organic materials under oxygen-free (anaerobic) conditions to produce a biogas.

backpressure turbine: a steam turbine that does not condense the steam as it exits the turbine so that low-pressure steam is available for use in other applications.

behind the meter: a reference to the electricity system that is located on the customer's side of the utility meter.

biogas: a combustible gas generated by an anaerobic digestion process that typically contains 50 to 70 percent methane, 30 to 50 percent CO_2, and small amounts of other gases.

bio-oil (also called pyrolysis oil): a liquid product created by decomposing wood in the absence of oxygen and condensing the resulting vapor. Fast pyrolysis processes produce a wood-derived bio-oil that looks similar to motor oil and has roughly 80,000 Btus per gallon.

boiler horsepower: equal to 33,478.8 Btus per hour (about 9809.5 W).

CHP: (see combined heat and power system)

cofiring: the simultaneous burning of biomass and a fossil fuel, usually coal, in the same burner.

cogeneration system: (see combined heat and power system)

combined heat and power system (CHP): a system that generates electricity and then recovers the waste heat from the generation process for useful purposes.

combustion (also called burning): a thermochemical process where a combustible material such as wood is heated to its ignition point in the presence of oxygen, causing it to decompose and burn. If adequate oxygen is provided, the process will continue until only ash (inorganic portion) is left.

condensing turbine: a steam turbine that has a condenser at its steam outlet.

direct combustion system: a method of combustion that burns wood in its solid form rather than gasifying or converting the wood into a liquid fuel before combustion takes place.

district heating system: a system that uses one or more central plants, e.g., a boiler, and distributes heat via pipes to two or more buildings to supply space heat or hot water for domestic use.

dry anaerobic digester (also called a high-solids digester): a type of anaerobic digester that uses a minimal amount of water, which allows smaller digesters to be as efficient as larger digesters. High-solids or "dry" anaerobic digesters are typically operated at a solids content of 35 percent.

extraction turbine: a steam turbine that removes (extracts) a portion of the steam as it flows through the turbine.

fast pyrolysis process: a thermochemical process where biomass materials are heated up to 750 to 1,000 °F in < 2 seconds in the absence of oxygen (so that combustion cannot occur), to cause wood to break down into gases, vapors, and char. The resulting vapors must also be condensed within 2 seconds in order to recover a pyrolysis oil (also called bio-oil) that looks similar to motor oil.

FBC system: (see fluidized bed combustion systems)

firetube boiler: boiler where the stack gases pass through boiler tubes that are surrounded by water.

fluidized bed combustion (FBC) systems: burner systems that combust wood fuel on a high-temperature bed of finely divided inert material, such as sand, that is agitated by air blown from beneath the bed.

fouling: the formation of mineral deposits on the surface of boiler tubes and other heat transfer surfaces. Deposits are formed from an abundance of minerals—primarily alkali metal salts—in the wood, which create chemical compounds that allow the ash to melt when the wood is combusted.

grate: a combustion chamber floor to support fuel, which can be inclined or horizontal and has openings to allow passage of air to aid in combustion and allow ash to fall through. Another type of grate is a wide moving chain across the bottom of the firebox that carries fuel through the combustion zone.

high-solids digester (also called a dry anaerobic digester): a type of anaerobic digester that uses a minimal amount of water, which allows smaller digesters to be as efficient as larger digesters. High-solids or "dry" anaerobic digesters are typically operated at a solids content of 35 percent.

ignition temperature: the temperature at which combustion will become self-sustaining if enough fuel and oxygen are available. For wood, the ignition temperature is in the range of 270 to 290 °F.

independent power plant: a generating plant operated by a nonutility that sells its power to a utility.

induction generator: a type of electricity generator that depends on the grid to supply voltage necessary to activate the generator's magnetic fields.

ligno-cellulose: materials that are primarily composed of cellulose, hemicellulose, and lignin. Typically, wood consists of 40 to 45 percent cellulose, 20 to 30 percent hemicellulose, and 20 to 30 percent lignin.

liquefaction process: a thermochemical process that occurs under high pressure in the absence of oxygen to produce a liquid fuel that has an energy content similar to diesel fuel.

mesophillic: refers to a family of micro-organisms that prefers to grow in temperatures of 95 to 105 °F or an anaerobic digestion system that operates at similar temperatures.

net metering: an arrangement that applies to customers of an electric power company that generate their own electricity and sell excess power to the utility. The customer pays or gets paid according to the net amount of electricity that flows back to the utility through his electric meter during each billing period. In some contracts, the amount a customer can sell back to the utility may be limited by law.

pile combustion system: a combustion system that burns wood fuel in either a heaped pile supported on horizontal or inclined grates, or in a thinly spread pile distributed across a traveling or stationary grate (see wet cell burner system).

process heat: heat used by industries for their manufacturing processes.

pulverized coal boiler: a boiler where coal is first reduced in size to a talcum powder consistency (pulverized) and then injected into the boiler so that it burns in suspension.

pyrolysis oil (also called bio-oil): a liquid product created by decomposing wood in the absence of oxygen and capturing and condensing the resulting vapor. Fast pyrolysis processes produce a wood-derived bio-oil that looks similar to motor oil and has roughly 80,000 Btus per gallon.

Rankine cycle: a process whereby steam is generated in a boiler and passed through a turbine to extract energy; then the steam exiting from the turbine is condensed and re-injected into the boiler, and the process is repeated.

reburning: a pollution control process whereby fuel is burned in the stack gases from a boiler under conditions of limited oxygen. The process converts nitrogen compounds in the stack gases into elemental nitrogen.

slagging: the formation of mineral deposits on the inside surface of combustion chambers. Deposits are formed from an abundance of minerals—primarily alkali metal salts—in certain types of wood, which create chemical compounds that allow the ash to melt when the wood is combusted.

slow pyrolysis: a thermochemical process that occurs with limited oxygen and is commonly used to make charcoal.

slurry digester: a type of anaerobic digester that stirs the mixture inside the digester to keep the solid particles mixed in the liquid. These designs are operated at a solids content of 4 to 20 percent.

spreader stoker: a device to meter and feed (stoke) fuel into a combustion device by spreading it across the grate or bottom of the firebox.

stoker: a method of feeding fuel to a burning device which may include using air to blow fuel into the combustion chamber, using augers to push fuel up from below the grate, mechanically spreading fuel onto a moving grate, or other methods.

suspension combustion system: a burner system using either air or centrifugal force to suspend wood particles during the combustion process.

synchronous generator: a type of electricity generator that has a control system associated with it that allows the generator to automatically follow the cycles of grid-generated electricity.

thermochemical process: a process that uses heat to cause chemical reactions that decompose biomass. One example of a thermochemical process involves heating wood above its ignition temperature in the presence of oxygen, causing it to burn.

thermophilic: refers to a family of micro-organisms that prefers to grow in temperatures of 125 to 135 °F or an anaerobic digestion system that operates at similar temperatures.

volatile solids: those solids in water or other liquids that are lost on ignition of dry solids at 550 °C (http://en.mimi.hu/environment/liquid.html).

watertube boiler: a type of boiler where water flows through the boiler's tubes and the stack gases are on the outside of the tubes.

wet cell burner system: a type of pile combustion system, usually consisting of a combustion chamber in the form of a vertical cylinder (see pile combustion system).

wood distillate: (see pyrolysis oil)

Chapter 5
The Economic Availability of Woody Biomass

Matthew Langholtz, Douglas R. Carter, and Richard Schroeder

INTRODUCTION

The primary sources of low-cost woody biomass in the southern wildland urban interface (WUI) include urban wood waste, logging residues, and small-diameter timber such as pulpwood. The economic availability of these resources is determined by a combination of procurement, harvesting, processing, and transportation costs, and it affects the economic feasibility of bioenergy generation projects. Here we describe an approach to develop local woody biomass resource supply curves to assess delivered costs to the bioenergy generation facility at different levels of demand.

BACKGROUND

Physical Supply Versus Economic Availability

Woody biomass resources available in the southern WUI, including urban wood waste, logging residues, and pulpwood, are described in chapter 2. An evaluation of the feasibility of bioenergy generation requires an assessment of not only physical availability but also the economic availability of woody biomass resources. A comprehensive economic assessment of multiple woody biomass resources takes into account that delivered costs vary with biomass type and distance or travel time, which is used to estimate travel costs. When transportation costs are taken into account, more costly resources in close proximity may be economically competitive with cheaper resources further away, and vice versa. As generation capacity and demand for woody biomass intensifies, increasingly expensive and distant resources may need to be purchased.

Supply Curves

A supply curve is a basic economic model used to describe and predict changes in the price and quantity of goods produced in competitive markets. A biomass resource supply curve is useful for estimating feedstock price at a given level of demand. **Figure 5.1** illustrates a hypothetical woody biomass resource supply curve. Quantity Q_1 can be generated at marginal price P_1 from urban wood waste, which is the cheapest resource because it is a zero- or negative-cost resource and widely available in the WUI. If biomass demand is increased due to higher levels of power generation capacity, more costly woody biomass resources, such as logging residues, might then be utilized to supply quantity Q_2 at price P_2. A more complex supply curve might include other available resources and would account for transportation cost in ranking the economic availability of these resources of different types at different travel times.

Depending on local conditions, utility companies may or may not offer a premium for biomass resources that are more expensive

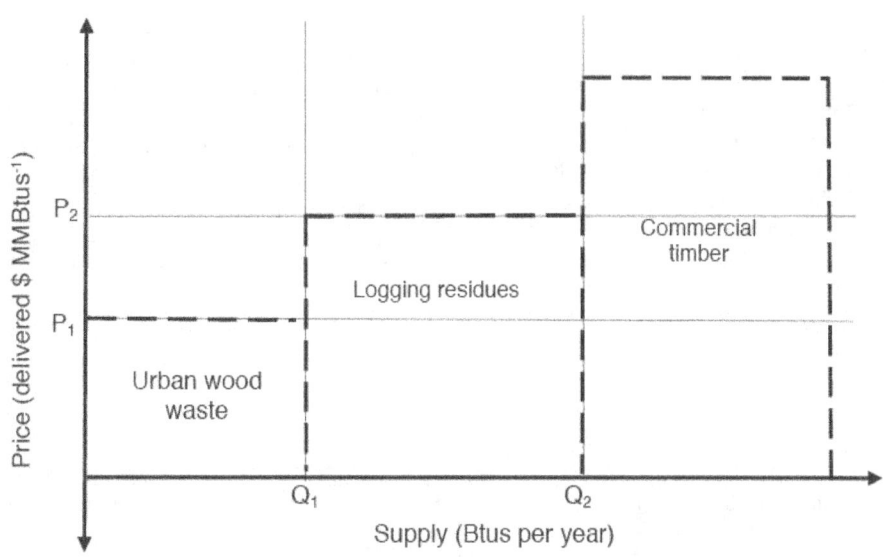

Figure 5.1—Hypothetical supply curve illustrating woody biomass resource categories.

or further away. If utilities can price discriminate, the total cost to the utility to meet a specified generation capacity is calculated as the area under the curve, or the sum of price multiplied by quantity for each resource category employed. In the example below, the calculation to purchase Q_2 with price discrimination is $(Q_1 * P_1) + (Q_2 * P_2)$. However, some utilities may not be able or willing to differentiate between different biomass resources that have different costs. If utilities cannot price discriminate, the total price to acquire a given resource is the maximum price times the total quantity. In the example below, this calculation to purchase Q_2 is $P_2 * Q_2$, which would result in a higher total cost to the utility.

Previous Biomass Supply Analyses

Biomass supply curves have been developed for large regions, which are appropriate for policy or macroeconomic analysis, and for local levels, which are needed to assess the economic viability of specific proposed bioenergy projects. National biomass supply curves suggest there are 268 million dry Mg (590 million green tons)[1] of agricultural waste, energy crops, forest residues, urban wood waste, and mill residues available in the United States annually. About 3 percent of this biomass is available at < $1.18/GJ[2] [$1.25 per million British thermal units (Btus[3])], which is close to the average price of coal sold to electric utilities in 2001 (Haq 2003). Regionally, the economic availability of pulpwood biomass was assessed for 62 forest survey units in the Southeastern United States. It was concluded that total delivered costs of production ranged from about $18 to $23/dry Mg ($8 to $10 per green ton) in low-cost areas (northeast Florida, southern Georgia, southern Alabama, and the Coastal Plain of South Carolina) and $33 to $75/dry Mg ($15 to $34 per green ton) in high-cost areas (south delta of Louisiana, Kentucky, West Virginia and the mountains of Tennessee, and Virginia) in 1987 dollars at production levels up to 45 350/dry Mg/year (100,000 green tons) (Young and others 1990, 1991). Delivered costs of biomass from dedicated feedstock supply systems (DFSSs) at various scales of analysis in the United States were estimated to range from < $22/dry Mg ($10 per green ton) to > $110/dry Mg ($50 per green ton) (Graham and others 1997, Walsh 1998). For localized assessments, a Geographic Information System (GIS)-based tool to estimate quantities and costs of forest thinnings and residues from timber management units has been developed for applications in northern California (Chalmers and others 2003). These previous works assess biomass availability at regional levels or are limited to biomass from commercial forestry.

METHODS

Developing localized woody biomass supply curves requires information about production costs and the physical availability of woody biomass resources in the area of interest. Here we describe our cost assumptions, the data used to estimate available woody biomass quantities, and methods to account for the spatial distribution of woody biomass resources.

Cost Assumptions

The delivered cost of woody biomass, as with conventional forest products, can be defined as a sum of procurement, harvest, transportation, and miscellaneous management costs. These costs vary with local operational conditions, and ideally should be assessed for specific sites. We assemble southernwide cost assumptions, which could be modified with the availability of site-specific cost information, and use a sensitivity analysis to assess the influence of increased production costs on the economic availability of woody biomass. The cost, operational, and wood density assumptions are described in this section and summarized in **tables 5.1, 5.2,** and **5.3.** Urban wood waste, logging residues, and other potential woody biomass resources are described in more detail in chapter 2.

Procurement cost—Procurement cost is the amount paid to gain ownership of a biomass resource. Procurement cost is equivalent to the term "stumpage price" in the forest industry, i.e., the price paid to a timber owner for the right to harvest. Urban wood wastes and logging residues are bound to have low procurement costs. Urban wood waste handlers in the Southeastern United States typically pay a tipping fee, or disposal fee. Disposal fees nationwide range from $94 to $22/dry Mg ($51 to $12 per green ton) for landfilled wood and $21 to $2/dry Mg ($11 to $1 per green ton) for processed wood (Wiltsee 1998). Tipping fees for urban wood in the South typically range from $33 to $55/dry Mg ($15 to $25 per green ton) delivered to a receiving area. This tipping fee translates into a negative procurement cost. Forest plantation owners pay postharvest site-preparation costs of about $462/ha ($186 per acre), including raking and piling of logging residues (Smidt and others 2005), and removal of logging residue reduces these site-preparation costs for replanting plantations (Watson and Stokes 1989). Therefore, logging residues also represent a liability to the owner and are available at no or low cost (Watson and others 1986a). In this analysis, we assume procurement costs of −$27.56/dry Mg (−$15 per green ton) for urban wood waste,

---

[1] Values are expressed as dry metric units followed by green imperial units. We assume moisture contents (green weight basis) of 37, 40, and 47 percent for logging residues, urban wood waste, and pulpwood, respectively, in our analysis, and assume 50 percent where not specified from referenced sources. The 37-percent moisture content assumption for logging residues assumes air drying and excludes leaves.

[2] GJ = gigajoule or 1 billion joules, 1 gigajoule = 0.9478 MM Btu or about 116 dry pounds of wood.

[3] 1 Btu = 1055 joules.

Table 5.1—Summary of cost assumptions for three woody biomass resources[a]

Cost Category	Urban wood waste	Logging residue	Pulpwood
	dollars dry/Mg (dollars per green ton)		
Procurement cost[b]	−27.56 (−15.00)	3.31 (1.89)	14.33 (6.89)
Harvest and process	33.07 (18.00)	26.46 (15.12)	26.46 (12.72)
Load and unload	2.28 (1.24)	2.06 (1.18)	1.91 (0.92)
One-way haul (per hour)	6.83 (3.72)	6.19 (3.54)	5.73 (3.12)
Example total delivered cost of a 1-hour haul[c]	21.45 (11.68)	44.21 (25.27)	54.16 (26.77)

[a] Details used in calculating the costs are shown in table 5.2.
[b] Negative costs for urban wood waste reflect disposal costs, known as "tipping fees."
[c] Equals the sum of two times the one-way haul cost and the remaining three cost categories.

Table 5.2—Operational assumptions

Variable/attribute	Logging residue	Urban wood waste	Pulpwood
Load and unload time per load (hours)	0.50	0.50	0.50
Load and unload cost per load (dollars)	25.00	25.00	25.00
Green tons per load	23.0	22.0	28.0
Load and unload cost per green ton (dollars)	1.09	1.14	0.89
Moisture content (green weight basis) (percent)	37	40	47
Ash content (percent)	5	5	2
Load and unload cost per dry ton (dollars)	1.87	2.07	1.73
Haul cost (dollars per hour per load)[a]	75.00	75.00	75.00
Haul cost (dollars per hour per green ton)	3.26	3.41	2.68
Two-way haul cost (dollars per hour per dry ton)	11.24	12.40	10.40
Million Btus per dry ton	15.58	15.58	16.15
Harvest and process (dollars per dry ton)	24.00	30.00	24.00
Procurement cost (dollars per dry ton)	3.00	(25.00)	13.00
Percent of quantity assumed recoverable	90	60	100

[a] Based on prices received from trucking companies accounting for varying fleet age, weight, and expenses.

Table 5.3—Wood density assumptions

Species category	Density
	g/cm^3 *(pounds per cubic foot)*
Hardwoods	0.513 (32)
Softwoods	0.481 (30)

which is estimated as an inexpensive tipping fee, and $3.31/dry Mg ($1.89 per green ton) for logging residues, based on typical procurement costs of $2 to $4/dry Mg ($1 to $2 per green ton) for logging residues in the South.[4]

A more expensive woody biomass resource that can be employed to meet demand beyond that available from waste resources is pulpwood. Pulpwood refers to small-diameter trees, typically 3.6 to 6.5 inches d.b.h., that are usually harvested for manufacturing paper. An estimated 93.0 million m³ (3.3 billion cubic feet) was harvested in the South in 2003 (Johnson 2003). For pulpwood to be economically competitive as a feedstock for energy, energy from the wood needs to be cheaper than energy from other sources (e.g., coal, natural gas, and solar energy) and the wood has to be offered a higher price for energy than for other uses (e.g., pulpwood [Sedjo 1997]). However, in conditions of low pulpwood stumpage prices and high biomass demand, some portion of this pulpwood supply could be allocated to bioenergy production (Perlack and others 2005). Southwide pine pulpwood

stumpage prices reported by Timber-Mart South ranged from $10 to $27/dry Mg ($5 to $13 per green ton) between 1995 and 2005, and averaged $13.62/dry Mg ($6.55 per green ton) over the four quarters of 2006. In this analysis, we assume pulpwood stumpage prices of $14.33/dry Mg ($6.89 per green ton). This estimate might be high because low-cost woody biomass from forest thinnings for habitat restoration, southern pine beetle control, timber stand improvement, and fuel load reduction (e.g., Bolding and Lanford 2001, Bolding and others 2003, Mason and others 2006, Meeker and others 2004, Rummer and others 2004, Watson and Stokes 1989) is likely to be purchased for bioenergy before it is necessary to buy merchantable pulpwood timber. Alternatively, if significant portions of pulpwood are required to meet demand, competition for pulpwood could drive prices higher. In a later sensitivity analysis, we increase procurement costs by 25 percent.

Harvest and processing costs—Harvest, processing, and transportation costs under various conditions are discussed in chapter 3. Harvest and transportation costs for urban wood waste and logging residues are typically higher than their procurement costs **(fig. 5.2)**. Forest residue harvesting operations can use conventional skidding equipment or specialized woody biomass harvesting technology, might be harvested during or after conventional harvesting operations, and might be chipped in woods or delivered unchipped, depending on site-specific conditions and forest management objectives. In various studies, stump-to-truck wood harvest technologies and costs ranged from $11 to $68/dry Mg ($5 to $31 per green ton) **(table 5.4)** (Bolding and Lanford 2001, Hartsough and others 1997, Rummer and

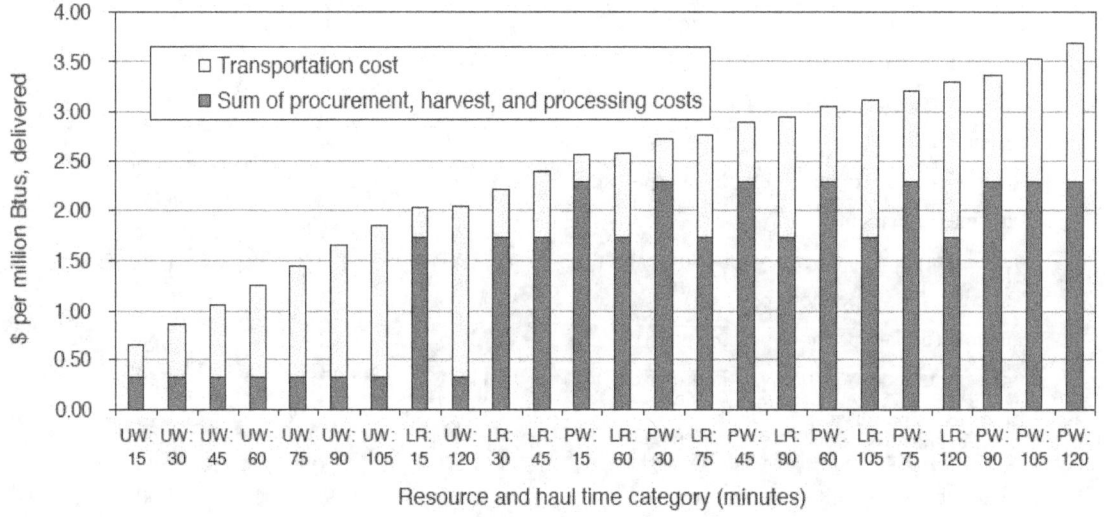

Figure 5.2—Transportation cost and sum of procurement, harvest, and processing costs of urban wood waste (UW), logging residues (LR), and pulpwood (PW) within a 2-hour haul travel time at 15-minute intervals. Transportation costs include loading and unloading costs.

---

[4] Personal communication. 2007. T. Harris, Publisher, Timber Mart-South, Center for Forest Business, Warnell School of Forestry and Natural Resources, University of Georgia, 180 E. Green Street, Athens, GA 30602-2152.

others 2004, Watson and Stokes 1989, Watson and others 1986b). Costs typically are lower for plantation conditions than for natural stands, are lower for higher density stands and larger tracts, and can be reduced by combining the harvest of commercial timber and residues in one operation. The cost of whole-tree chips loaded into a trailer in the woods (hardwood and softwood) ranged from $23.85 to $32.37/dry Mg ($13.63 to $18.50 per green ton), including stumpage which typically cost $1 to $2 per green ton (Timber Mart-South 2006). On a dry weight basis, these costs would be increased for pulpwood having a higher moisture content, though they would be decreased on a green weight basis in a single-pass, whole-tree chipping operation. The cost of processing (chipping) urban wood waste varies, ranging from $14.20 to $60.63/dry Mg ($6.45 to $27.50 per green ton) in 2006 Florida bids. In this analysis, we use harvest and chipping costs of $26.46/dry Mg ($15.12 per green ton) for logging residues and pulpwood and $33.07/dry Mg ($18 per green ton) for urban wood waste. We then measure the impact of increasing these costs 25 percent.[5] Other detailed assumptions applied in this analysis are shown in tables 5.1, 5.2, and 5.3.

Table 5.4—Summary of published harvest costs (stump to truck)

Year	Author	Region	Operation	Product[a]	Cost	Equivalent 2005[b]
					---- $/dry Mg ($ per green ton) ----	
2004	Rummer and others	West	Bundling	EW	23.18 (10.50)[c]	24.58 (11.15)
2001	Bolding and Lanford	Southeast	Cut-to-length harvesting with small in-woods chipper	RW	17.13 (7.77)	17.68 (8.02)
				EW	27.65 (12.54)	28.55 (12.95)
1994	Hartsough and others	California	Whole tree (plantation)	EW	16.42 (7.45)	14.20 (6.44)
			Hybrid (plantation)	EW	12.02 (5.45)	10.38 (4.71)
			Cut-to-length (plantation)	EW	37.70 (17.10)	32.61 (14.79)
			Whole tree (natural stand)	EW	22.05 (10.00)	19.07 (8.65)
			Hybrid (natural stand)	EW	27.67 (12.55)	23.94 (10.86)
			Cut-to-length (natural stand)	EW	57.76 (26.20)	49.98 (22.67)
1989	Watson and others	Alabama/ Mississippi	Preharvest (plantation)	EW	32.19–34.83 (14.60–15.80)	56.88–61.60 (25.80–27.94)
		Mississippi	Preharvest (natural)	EW	33.38–35.74 (15.14–16.21)	58.97–135.80 (26.75–28.65)
		Alabama	Integrated (plantation)	EW	22.29 (10.11)	39.40 (17.87)
1986	Watson and others	Southeast	Conventional (52-percent removal)	RW	13.78–22.27 (6.25–10.10)	33.64–54.39 (15.26–24.67)
			One-pass (85-percent removal)	EW	18.30–22.38 (8.30–10.15)	44.69–54.65 (20.27–24.79)
			Two-pass (76-percent removal)	EW	26.70–28.00 (12.11–12.70)	65.19–68.43 (29.57–31.04)

[a] EW = energy wood; RW = roundwood.
[b] Adjusted for inflation using the Bureau of Labor Statistics Produce Price Index for softwood logs and bolts to September of 2005 [http://data.bls.gov

---

[5] The cost of diesel fuel makes up approximately 25 percent of the total harvest and process cost. Increasing total harvest and process costs by 25 percent simulates a scenario in which the price of diesel is doubled.

Transportation costs—Transportation costs vary with fuel price, travel time, road condition, biomass density, and handling characteristics, and can be 50 percent or more of the total delivered cost (see chapter 3). Mean roundtrip biomass transportation costs in Tennessee within an 80-km (50-mile) haul have been estimated at $8 to $18/dry Mg ($4 to $8 per green ton) (Graham and others 1997) and about $13/dry Mg ($6 per green ton) for haul distances of 97 km (60 miles) in Mississippi (Mitchell 2006). Transportation costs have been estimated on a per km basis at 0.11cents/dry Mg/km (0.08 cents per green ton per mile) for short-rotation woody crops in Florida (Langholtz 2005) and ranging from 0.14 to 0.21 cents/dry Mg/km (0.10 to 0.15 cents per green ton per mile) for the Southeast (Rummer 2006). Hauling on roads with low speed limits increases transportation cost, and particularly affects overall costs of low-value wood products (Grebner and others 2005). To calculate transportation cost as a function of road conditions (see "Haul Time Calculations" below), we estimate transportation cost as a function of transportation time rather than distance. Based on the operational assumptions for each resource shown in table 5.2, we assume one-way transportation costs to be $7.52, $7.19, and $5.91/dry Mg/hour ($3.41, $3.26, and $2.68 per green ton per hour) for urban wood waste, logging residues, and pulpwood, respectively. We then double these values to account for return trips with empty loads, and add $1.85 to $1.90/dry Mg (0.89 cents to $1.14 per green ton) to account for loading and unloading. These values are conservative compared to the hauling rate of 0.16 cents/dry Mg/km (0.12 cents per green ton per loaded mile) reported by Timber Mart-South for the fourth quarter of 2006. In a sensitivity analysis, we increase total transportation costs by 30 percent.[6]

Total cost by resource-haul time category—Based on the above cost assumptions, we calculate the delivered cost of each woody biomass resource within a given haul time at 15-minute increments. We feel this approach most accurately reflects site-specific variation in road networks, speed limits, and geographical constraints. By ranking these resources from lowest cost to highest cost, we estimate the progression of most to least economically available woody biomass resources, accounting for travel time from the point of delivery. **Table 5.5** illustrates how, under these cost assumptions, urban wood waste requiring a one-way haul up to 105 minutes is cheaper than other woody biomass resources with shorter haul times. Transportation costs make up 10 to 84 percent of total delivered costs, depending on the resource type and travel time (fig. 5.2). Costs could alternatively be calculated by haul distance rather than time, or transportation cost could be assumed uniform for each woody biomass resource within a maximum haul radius. The next step in constructing the woody biomass resource supply curve is to determine what quantity of

biomass is available in each woody biomass resource-haul time category for a given community.

Physical Availability

In addition to production costs, information about the physical availability of resources is required to construct supply curves. We compile county-level woody biomass resource information for all counties in the Southern United States. To estimate woody biomass quantities from logging residues and pulpwood, we accessed Timber Product Output (TPO) reports (http://srsfia2.fs.fed.us/php/tpo2/tpo.php) maintained by the Forest Service, Southern Research Station (SRS), Forest Inventory and Analysis Research Work Unit (FIA). This database provides forest inventory and harvest information, including annual yields of logging residues and pulpwood at the county level. The SRS derives these values by updating FIA harvest data with regional harvest information based on mill surveys.[7] This information is useful because it estimates actual rather than potential logging residue and roundwood yields. Where potential woodsheds expand beyond the 13 Southern States and SRS TPO data are unavailable, we use data from the nationwide Timber Products Output Mapmaker Version 1.0 (http://ncrs2.fs.fed.us/4801/timberproducts/index.htm), which uses the most recent available FIA inventory for each State. FIA allows a maximum error of 5 percent per 1 billion cubic feet of growing stock on timberland at the State level. Errors are higher at the county level. See http://fia.fs.fed.us/tools-data/other/default.asp for more information.

Because the pulpwood harvest identified in the FIA TPO report is currently used to produce pulp and paper products, not all of this resource is economically available for bioenergy. However, additional biomass is available from forest thinnings (Condon and Putz, in press; Perlack and others 2005), which is not included in this assessment. Furthermore, southwide softwood and hardwood growth exceeds removals (Adams and others 2003), indicating that more wood can be sustainably harvested. Recent trends of poor stumpage prices and loss of markets for forest products in the South may have reduced forest management activities (Smidt and others 2005), which could be mitigated by providing additional timber markets.

We assume 0.111 dry Mg (0.244 green tons) of urban wood waste per capita annually (based on an average of 0.203 green tons at 40-percent moisture content reported by Wiltsee 1998). Wiltsee's study of 30 metropolitan areas across the United States showed relative consistency per capita nationwide; values tended to be higher in Southern States. This per capita estimate includes municipal solid waste wood from yard waste and tree trimmings but excludes an additional 0.1 dry Mg (0.2 green tons) per capita

---

[6] The price of diesel is approximately 30 percent of the cost of operating a tractor trailer. Increasing total transportation costs simulates a scenario in which the price of diesel is doubled.

[7] Personal communication. 2007. Tony Johnson, Section Head of Resource Use, USDA Forest Service, Southern Research Station, Forest Inventory and Analysis, 4700 Old Kingston Pike, Knoxville, TN 37919.

per year reported from industrial wood, e.g., cabinet and pallet production, and construction and demolition debris. We multiply this average annual per capita yield by county level 2005 U.S. Census population estimates (www.census.gov/popest/counties/) to estimate total annual county yield of urban wood waste. We then use the method described below to estimate what portion of these county-level resources are within each resource-haul time category for a given delivery point.

Haul Time Calculations

GIS is a useful tool for identifying possible locations for bioenergy facilities (e.g., Young and others 1991); scheduling harvests of biomass resources (e.g., Chalmers and others 2003); and calculating transportation costs within woodsheds (e.g., Brewington and others 2001). We use GIS to calculate travel costs based on existing road infrastructure for each community and to assess the proportion of each county within a given haul time category. We assign speed limits to road features and divide road lengths by speed limits to estimate travel time. We increase haul time by 25 percent to account for operational delays and rerouting for bridges with gross vehicle weights < 36 Mg (40 tons), use ArcGIS® network analyst to calculate service areas based on travel time, and calculate the proportion of each county in each haul time category in 15-minute intervals. See text box below and Langholtz and others (2006) for more information about the use of ArcGIS® network analyst in this analysis. Rough estimates of woody biomass availability in each haul time category could be made using simpler techniques.

Supply Curve Construction

After collecting information regarding quantities, distribution, and costs for each woody biomass resource, supply curves can be constructed. Assuming homogeneous distribution of woody biomass resources within counties (a necessary assumption given the FIA source data), we calculate the amount of woody biomass in each haul time category in each county, and then summarize quantities available from each resource-haul time category for the area of interest. We then assign total delivered costs for each resource-haul time category, and sort from least to most expensive (table 5.5). Supply curves are then plotted where the x axis is the cumulative total amount of woody biomass with each additional resource-haul time category and the y axis is total delivered cost. Curves can be plotted as an Excel® scatter plot or by using the Macro Economic Supply Curve Chart Excel® add-in. We express units based on energy content of the biomass, though units could be expressed as mass. See **figure 5.3** for the steps used in constructing the woody biomass resource supply curves.

Assessing transportation cost based on haul time rather than distance accounts for road infrastructure in a woodshed. Haul times can be estimated by using GIS to account for speed limits assigned to U.S. Census Topologically Integrated Geographic Encoding and Referencing (TIGER) road layers. Following is a summary of steps that can be used to assess haul times by generating service areas with ArcGIS® Network Analyst:

1. *Identify delivery point (county centroid, generation plant, etc.).*

2. *Identify area of interest (AOI) to include the maximum potential extent of the woodshed. A 450-km (280-mile) radius includes more than a 4-hour one-way haul. Identify counties within the AOI.*

3. *Download U.S. Census TIGER roads shapefiles for the AOI from http://arcdata.esri.com/data/tiger2000/tiger_download.cfm. Merge the roads, define the projection (see Price and Coleman 2003), and reproject the merged roads layer. Keep all layers in the same projection.*

4. *Assign speed limits to each roads segment according to census feature class codes and calculate travel time (see Price and Price 2003). To account for expected travel delays, we increase calculated travel times by 25 percent.*

5. *Calculate service areas based on haul time using the ArcGIS® Network Analyst Service Area Calculator (see Chandrasekhar 2005). We assess haul times based on 15-minute haul intervals, and assume the "ToBreak" field value for each haul time category. Export service area polygons to a shapefile.*

6. *Union the service area polygons to the counties polygons and clip as necessary. Ensure the unioned shapefile is projected, add a "NewArea" field (float), and calculate areas of each feature.*

7. *Add a "ConcCat" field (text) and concatenate the county name or "FIPS" field with the "ToBreak" field. Summarize the "ConCat" field including the average of the original area and the sum of the "NewArea" field.*

8. *Import the summarized *.dbf to a spreadsheet software such as Excel®. For each "FIPS-ToBreak" record, divide the "NewArea" by the original area to determine what percentage of each county is in each haul time category.*

9. *This percentage can be used to estimate what percentage of the woody biomass resource in each county resides in each haul time category. A Microsoft Excel® Pivot Table can then be used to summarize the estimated total of each biomass resource in each haul time category.*

Table 5.5—The 10 least expensive woody biomass resource-haul time categories within a 2-hour haul travel time ranked from least to most expensive (costs account for ash content)

Resource	Haul time category (*minutes*)	*$/dry Mg ($ per green ton)*	*$/GJ ($ per million Btu)*
Urban wood waste	0–15	11.21 (6.10)	0.62 (0.65)
Urban wood waste	15–30	14.62 (7.96)	0.81 (0.85)
Urban wood waste	30–45	18.04 (9.82)	1.00 (1.05)
Urban wood waste	45–60	21.45 (11.68)	1.19 (1.25)
Urban wood waste	60–75	24.87 (13.54)	1.37 (1.45)
Urban wood waste	75–90	28.29 (15.40)	1.56 (1.65)
Urban wood waste	90–105	31.70 (17.26)	1.75 (1.85)
Logging residues	0–15	34.93 (19.96)	1.92 (2.03)
Urban wood waste	105–120	35.12 (19.12)	1.93 (2.04)
Logging residues	15–30	38.03 (21.73)	2.09 (2.21)

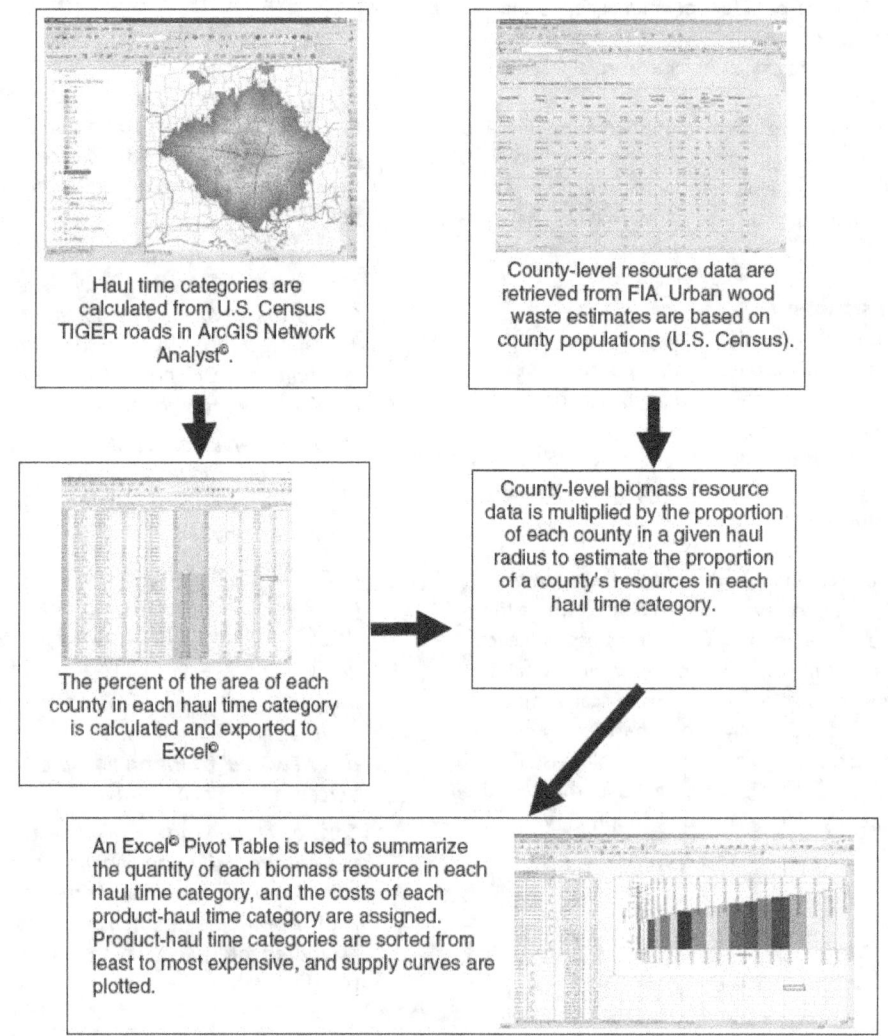

Figure 5.3—Work flow diagram illustrating resources and steps used in woody biomass resource supply curve construction.

RESULTS

Twenty-eight counties were selected in the WUI of the 13 Southern States as having potential for using woody biomass for energy generation (the county selection process is described in chapter 6 and selected States are shown in chapter 6, fig. 6.2). Approximate conversions of trillion Btus to MW, dry tons per year, truckloads per year, and homes powered per year are shown on the scales in **figure 5.4.** For the 28 counties, there was an average of 2.4, 9.1, and 18.0 trillion Btus of urban wood waste,

logging residues, and pulpwood, respectively, within a 2-hour haul distance. Relative economic availability of woody biomass among the counties varies with quantity supplied. For example, of the 28 counties assessed, results suggest Le Flore County, OK, has the highest marginal cost, i.e., cost of an additional unit, of biomass at quantities up to 7 trillion Btus, while Trimble County in Kentucky shows the highest marginal costs at demand above this amount (**fig. 5.5**). Typical demand is likely to be in the range of 2.3 to 4.7 T Btus to produce about 20 to 40 MW of electricity, enough to

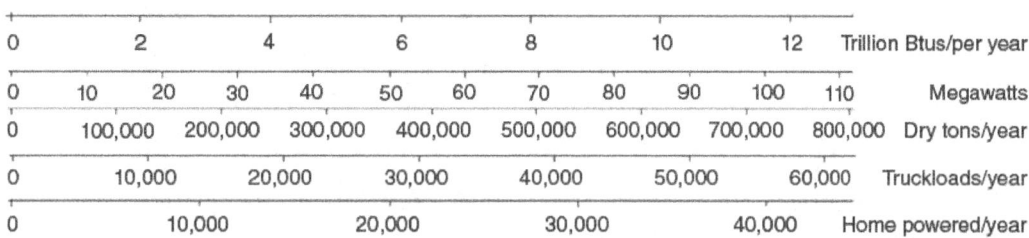

Figure 5.4—Scale showing general relationship between Btus per year, MW, dry tons of biomass per year, truckloads of biomass per year, and homes powered per year. Values are calculated based on 8.6 MW/trillion Btus (see chapter 6, table 6.2), 16 million Btus per dry ton of biomass, 23 green tons of biomass per truckload, and 400 homes powered per MW considering typical consumption in the South (Bellemar 2003). The actual proportions between these values vary with generating efficiency, moisture content, household energy consumption, and other factors.

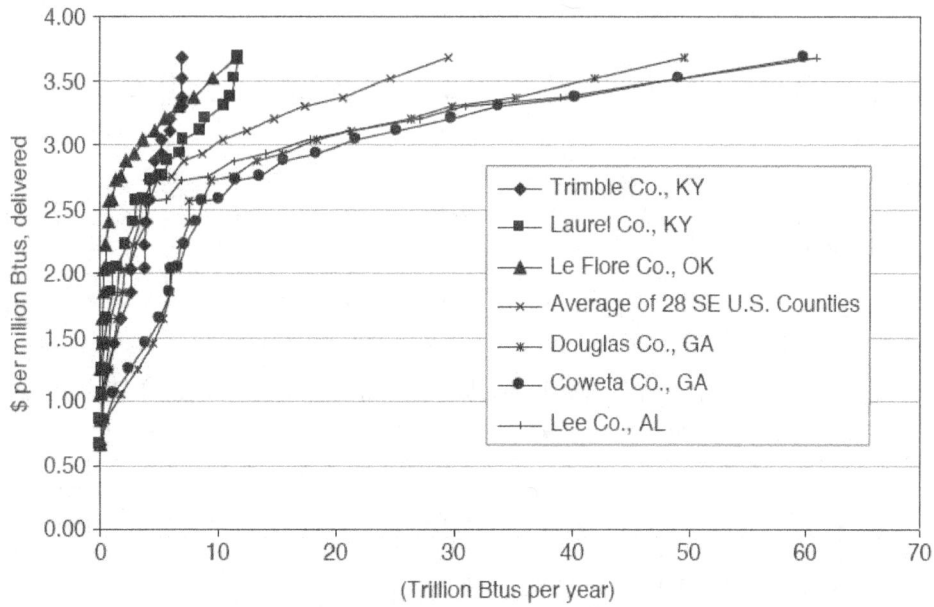

Figure 5.5—Example of low, high, and average woody biomass supply curves of selected WUI counties. Biomass sources include urban wood waste, logging residues, and pulpwood within a 2-hour haul distance. The average supply curve includes 2.4, 9.1, and 18.0 trillion Btus of urban wood waste, logging residues, and pulpwood, respectively. Approximate conversions of trillion Btus to MW, dry tons per year, truckloads per year, and homes powered per year are shown on the scales in figure 5.4.

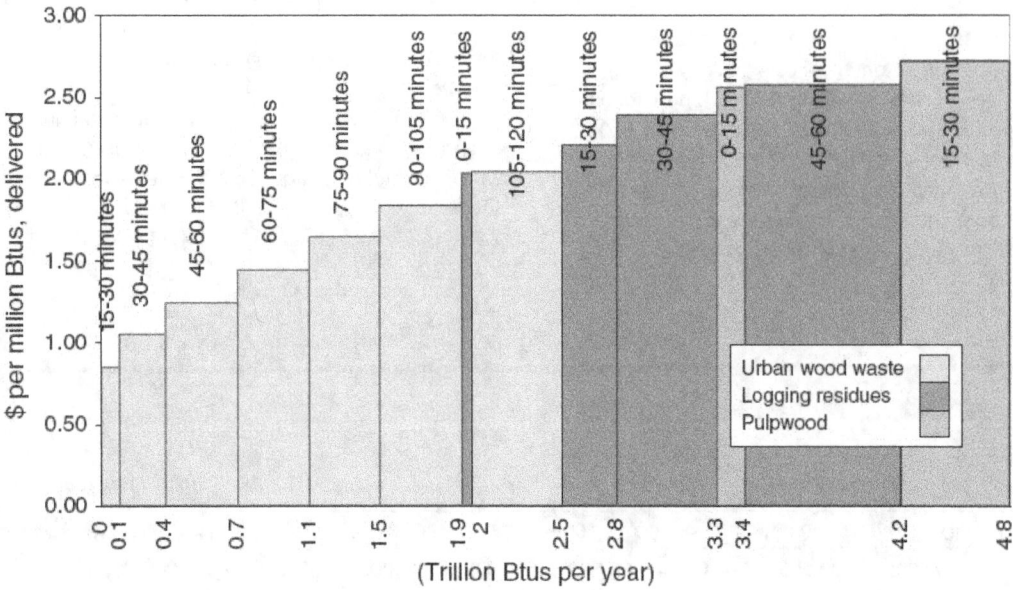

Figure 5.6—Prices, quantities, and resource-haul category composition up to 4.8 trillion Btus, based on the average of 28 selected counties in the WUI. Approximate conversions of trillion Btus to MW, dry tons per year, truckloads per year, and homes powered per year are shown on the scales in figure 5.4.

power 8,000 to 16,000 households in the South (Bellemar 2003). Quantities in this range cost $1.93 to $2.58/GJ ($2.04 to $2.72 per million Btu) for the 28-county average cost curve. Under the average curve, demand up to 4.8 trillion Btus can be met with urban wood residues within a 2-hour haul, logging residues within a 1-hour haul, and pulpwood within a 30-minute haul (**fig. 5.6**).

Biomass literature typically suggests a maximum transportation distance of about 80 km (50 miles) for bioenergy to be economically viable. However, the supply curve in figure 5.6 indicates that urban wood waste 105 minutes away, or about 113 km (70 miles) away, can outcompete closer, more expensive resources. Limiting potential woody biomass resources to those available within a 1-hour haul radius excludes resources that might otherwise be available, and shows pulpwood at a 15-minute haul time to be cheaper than logging residues at a 1-hour haul time for the 28-county average curve (**figs. 5.7 and 5.8**). Excluding woody biomass resources beyond a 1-hour haul time shows a more conservative assessment of the economic availability of woody biomass to a community by reducing the area of the woodshed.

Such a scenario might be indicative of conditions under increased competing demand spurred by multiple bioenergy generation facilities in a region.

We ran a sensitivity analysis to assess the impact of increasing costs on the economic availability of woody biomass resources. The analysis includes: (1) increasing procurement costs to $−20.67, $4.13, and $17.91/dry Mg ($11.25, $2.36, and $8.61 per green ton) for urban wood waste, logging residues, and pulpwood, respectively; (2) increasing harvest and process costs by 25 percent; (3) increasing load and transportation costs by 30 percent; and (4) adding all of these cost increases. Because each type of cost increase affects the three resources differently, the resource-haul time category ranking from lowest cost to highest cost changes slightly. Cumulative impacts of all three cost increases range from 0.52 cents per million Btus for logging residues at a 15-minute haul time to $1.40 per million Btus for urban wood waste at a 2-hour haul time, and vary by resource-haul time category (**fig. 5.9**). Increasing transportation costs has a greater impact at longer travel times.

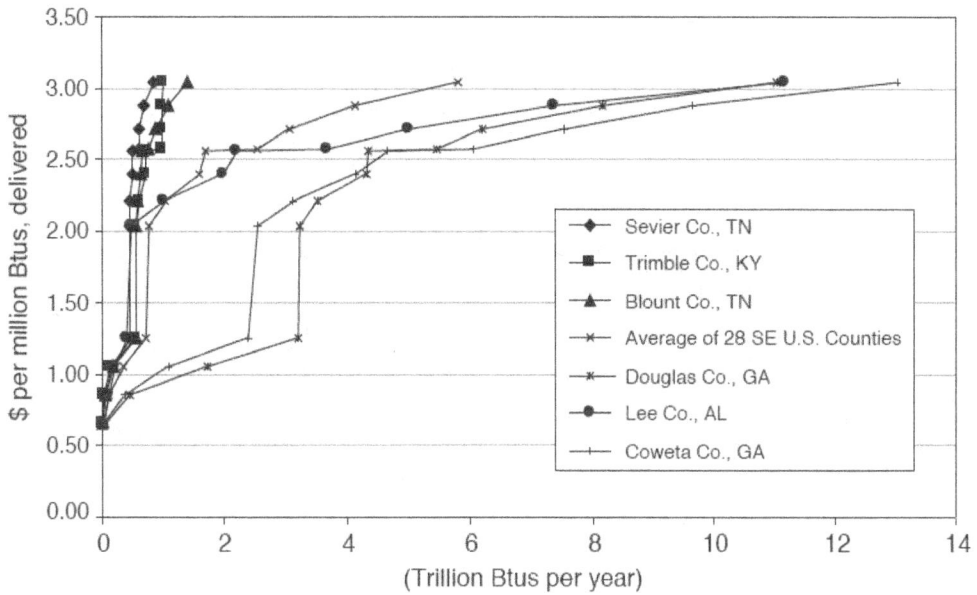

Figure 5.7—Example of low, high, and average woody biomass supply curves of selected WUI counties. Sources include urban wood waste, logging residues, and pulpwood within a 1-hour haul radius. The average supply curve includes 0.7, 1.7, and 3.4 trillion Btus of urban wood waste, logging residues, and pulpwood, respectively, as shown in figure 5.8. Approximate conversions of trillion Btus to MW, dry tons per year, truckloads per year, and homes powered per year are shown on the scales in figure 5.4.

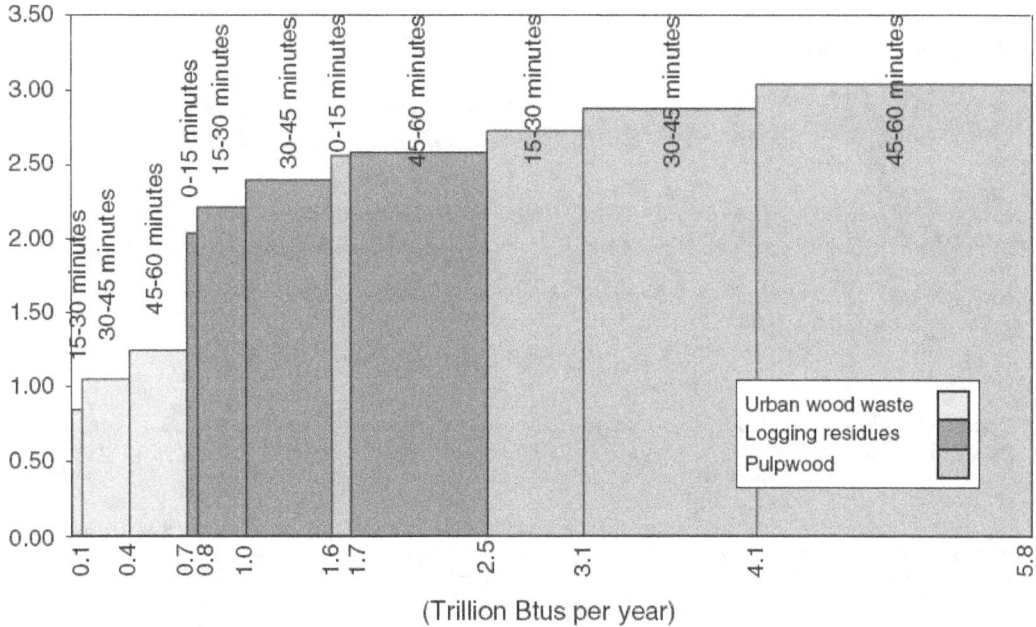

Figure 5.8—Prices, quantities, and resource-haul category composition within a 1-hour haul distance, based on the average of 28 southern counties in the WUI. Approximate conversions of trillion Btus to MW, dry tons per year, truckloads per year, and homes powered per year are shown on the scales in figure 5.4.

(A)

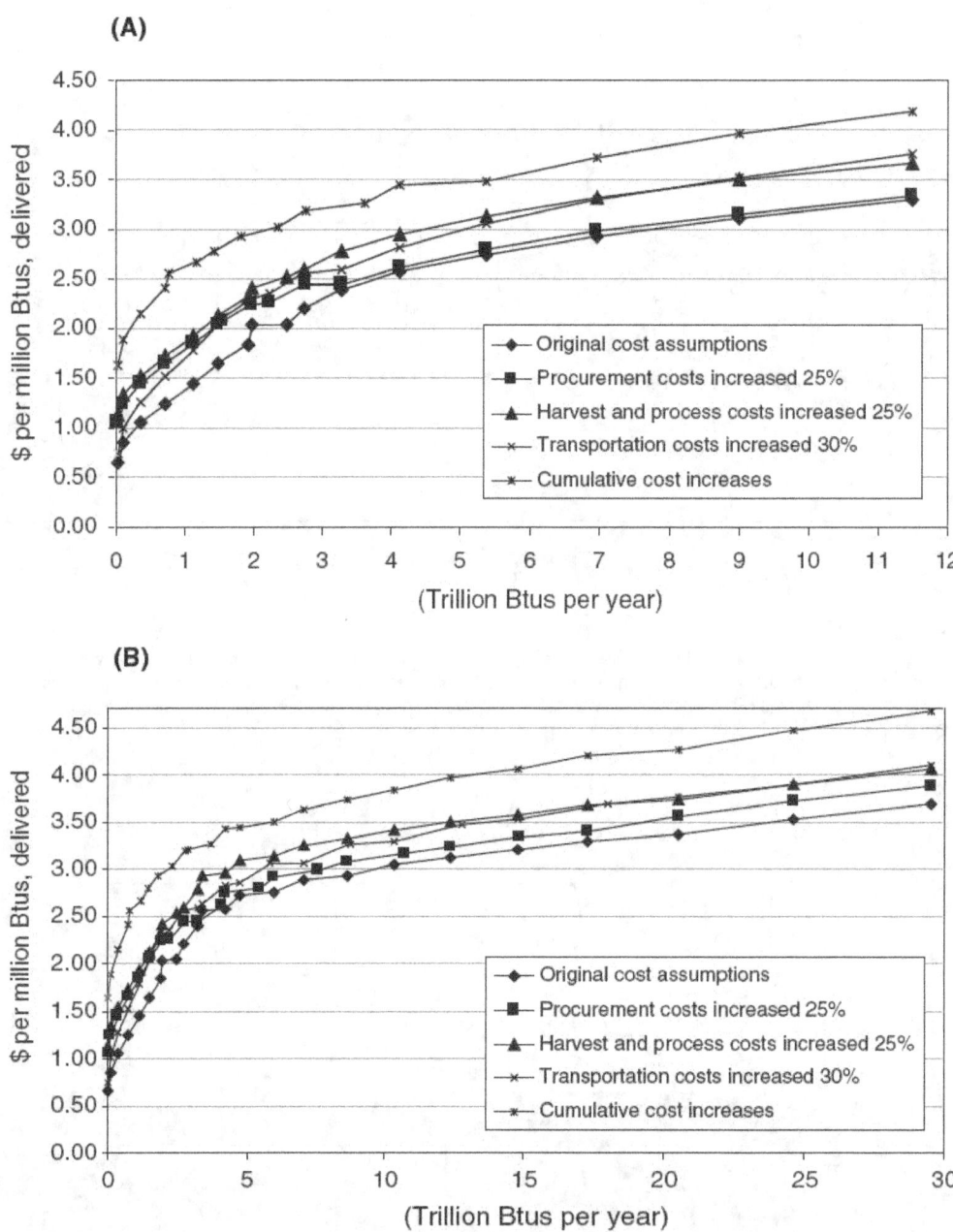

(B)

Figure 5.9—Average supply curves of 28 southern WUI counties: (A) including 2.4 and 9.1 trillion Btus of urban wood waste and logging residues within a 2-hour haul distance, and (B) including an additional 18.0 trillion Btus of pulpwood within a 2-hour haul distance. Curves represent (1) original cost assumptions; (2) procurement costs increased to −$20.67, $4.13, and $17.91/dry Mg (−$11.25, $2.36, and $8.61 per green ton) for urban wood waste, logging residues, and pulpwood, respectively; (3) harvest and process costs increased 25 percent; (4) load and transportation costs increased 30 percent; and (5) the sum of all cost increases. Approximate conversions of trillion Btus to MW, dry tons per year, truckloads per year, and homes powered per year are shown on the scales in figure 5.4.

CONCLUSIONS AND RECOMMENDED FUTURE RESEARCH

These supply curves illustrate local economic availability of woody biomass resources and prices that might be paid as a function of demand. Conclusions and stipulations include the following:

- On average for the 28 counties included in this study, up to 3.3 trillion Btus of woody biomass are typically available at < $2.27/GJ ($2.39 per million Btus) in WUI communities in the Southeastern United States. This biomass consists of urban wood waste within a 2-hour haul and logging residues within a 45-minute haul.
- Low-cost biomass resources, such as urban wood waste within a haul time of 2 hours or about 130 km (80 miles), can be cheaper than pulpwood and other resources available with shorter travel times.
- Woody biomass resources will become more expensive if multiple bioenergy efforts increase demand or when oil prices rise. Average maximum prices up to 4.0 trillion Btus are projected to increase to $2.73/GJ ($2.88 per million Btus) if the maximum haul radius is constrained to 1 hour and up to $3.44/GJ ($3.63 per million Btus) if, in addition, all assumed price increases are applied.
- Pulpwood resources included in this analysis assume current market prices. However, competing demand for this resource may increase prices.
- Opportunities may exist to use the cheapest woody biomass within a 2-hour haul radius to streamline bioenergy generation systems in anticipation of future reduced woodsheds resulting from increased competing demand.

Possible topics for future research include analysis of short- and long-run pulpwood supply and price impacts from alternative demand scenarios, alternative modes of transportation including rail and barge, potential woody biomass sources such as forest thinnings and DFSS, the use of hurricane debris for bioenergy generation, the impacts of hurricanes on the availability and sustainability of woody biomass, the impacts of forest industry and land use trends on the availability of woody biomass, and compensation for CO_2 mitigation or other incentives for renewable energy. Given higher resolution data from remote sensing, a more robust approach could be used to account for intracounty distribution of woody biomass resources. Because assumptions made in this analysis may not reflect local conditions, a decision support system could be developed to account for site-specific information for localized assessments.

REFERENCES

Adams, D.M.; Alig, R.; Brooks, D. [and others]. 2003. An analysis of the timber situation in the United States: 1952 to 2050. PNW–GTR–560. Portland, OR: U.S. Department of Agriculture Forest Service, Pacific Northwest Research Station. 254 p.

Bellemar, D. 2003. What is a megawatt? http://www.utilipoint.com/issuealert/article.asp?id=1728. [Date accessed: July 13, 2006].

Bolding, C.; Lanford, B. 2001. Forest fuel reduction through energy wood production using a small chipper/CLT harvesting system. Corvallis, OR: Oregon State University: 65–70.

Bolding, C.; Lanford, B.; Kellogg, L.D. 2003. Forest fuel reduction: current methods and future possibilities. In: Proceedings of the 2003 Council on Forest Engineering. Bar Harbor, ME: [Publisher unknown]: 5–10.

Brewington, R.; Williams, R.; Earl, J. 2001. Travel cost model for determining procurement zones using GIS. In: Hardwoods - an underdeveloped resource? Monticello, AR: Arkansas Forest Resource Center: 144–147.

Chalmers, S.; Hartsough, B.; DeLasaux, M. 2003. A GIS-based tool for estimating supply curves for forest thinnings and residues to biomass energy facilities in California. WRBEP Contract 55044. Final Report. University of California-Davis. Department of Biological and Agricultural Engineering. 10 p.

Chandrasekhar, T. 2005. ArcGIS® network analyst tutorial. Redlands, CA: ESRI. 38 p.

Condon, B.; Putz, F.E. [In press]. Countering the broadleaf invasion: financial and carbon consequences of removing hardwoods during longleaf pine savanna restoration. Restoration Ecology.

Graham, R.L.; Liu, W.; Downing, M. [and others]. 1997. The effect of location and facility demand on the marginal cost of delivered wood chips from energy crops: a case study of the State of Tennessee. Biomass and Bioenergy. 13(3): 117–123.

Grebner, D.; Grace, L.; Stuart, W. [and others]. 2005. A practical framework for evaluating hauling costs. International Journal of Forest Engineering. 16(2): 115–128.

Haq, Z. 2003. Biomass for electricity generation. http://www.eia.doe.gov/oiaf/analysispaper/biomass/. [Date accessed: June 15, 2006].

Hartsough, B.; Drews, E.; McNeel, J. [and others]. 1997. Comparison of mechanized systems for thinning ponderosa pine and mixed conifer stands. Forest Products Journal. 47(11/12): 59–68.

Johnson, T. 2003. Timber product output report [Internet database]. http://srsfia2.fs.fed.us/php/tpo2/tpo.php. [Date accessed: June 28, 2006].

Langholtz, M. 2005. Economic and environmental analysis of tree crops on marginal lands in Florida. University of Florida. 155 p. Ph.D. dissertation.

Langholtz, M.; Carter, D.; Marsik, M. [and others]. 2006. Measuring the economics of biofuel availability. ArcUser. October–December: 22–25.

Mason, C.L.; Lippke, B.R.; Zobrist, K.W. [and others]. 2006. Investments in fuel removals to avoid forest fires result in substantial benefits. Journal of Forestry. 104(1): 27–31.

Meeker, J.; Dixon, W.; Foltz, J. [and others]. 2004. Southern pine beetle, *Dendroctonus frontalis* Zimmermann. EENY–176. Gainesville, FL: IFAS. 3 p.

Mitchell, D. 2006. Case study of a biomass chipping operation on national forest land. In: Smallwood '06 conference. Madison, WI: U.S. Department of Agriculture Forest Service, Forest Products Laboratory. 30 p.

Perlack, R.; Wright, L.; Turhollow, A.F. [and others]. 2005. Biomass as feedstock for a bioenergy and bioproducts industry: the technical feasibility of a billion-ton annual supply. ORNL/TM–2005/66. Oak Ridge, TN: Oak Ridge National Laboratory. 78 p.

Price, M.; Coleman, R. 2003. Taming TIGER data: create emergency management maps using census 2000 data. ArcUser. January–March: 52–55.

Price, M.; Price, J. 2003. Coverage assessment using census 2000 TIGER roads. ArcUser. July–September: 54–58.

Rummer, B. 2006. Mechanized fuel reduction case studies. In: North Carolina wood energy conference. Raleigh, NC: North Carolina State University.

Rummer, B.; Len, D.; O'Brien, O. 2004. Forest residues bundling project-new technologies for residue removal. Auburn, AL: U.S. Department of Agriculture Forest Service, Southern Research Station, Forest Operations Unit. 20 p.

Sedjo, R.A. 1997. The economics of forest-based biomass supply. Energy Policy. 25(6): 559–566.

Smidt, M.; Silveira Folegatti, B.; Dubois, M. 2005. Costs and cost trends for forestry practices in the South. Forest Landowner. 64(2): 25–31.

Timber Mart-South. 2006. Quarterly market reports. Athens, GA: University of Georgia, Warnell School of Forest Resources, Center for Forest Business. 5 p.

U.S. Dept. of Commerce, B. o. t. C. (2000). "United States census 2000." http://www.census.gov/population/socdemo/migration/. [Date accessed: July 27, 2005].

Walsh, M.E. 1998. U.S. bioenergy crop economic analyses: status and needs. Biomass and Bioenergy. 14(4): 341–350.

Watson, W.; Ragan, J.; Straka, T. [and others]. 1986a. Economic analysis of potential fuelwood sources. In: Forests, the world and the profession: Proceedings of the 1986 Society of American Foresters national convention. Birmingham, AL: Society of American Foresters: 339-342.

Watson, W.; Stokes, B. 1989. Harvesting small trees and forest residues. In: X. Auburn, AL: U.S. Department of Agriculture Forest Service, Southern Forest Experiment Station: 131–139.

Watson, W.F.; Stokes, B.J.; Savelle, I.W. 1986b. Comparisons of two methods of harvesting biomass for energy. Forest Products Journal. 36(4): 63–68.

Wiltsee, G. 1998. Urban wood waste resource assessment. Golden, CO: National Renewable Energy Laboratory. 177 p.

Young, T.M.; Ostermeier, D.M.; Thomas, J.D. [and others]. 1990. A validation study of the industrial fuel chip supply simulator (IFCHIPS). Muscle Shoals, AL: U.S. Department of Energy. 82 p.

Young, T.M.; Ostermeier, D.M.; Thomas, J.D. [and others]. 1991. The economic availability of woody biomass for the Southeastern United States. Bioresource Technology. 37(1): 7–15.

Glossary of Terms

Btu: British thermal unit or 1,055.06 joules

DFSS: Dedicated feedstock supply system

FIA: Forest Inventory and Analysis of USDA Forest Service

GIS: Geographical information system

GJ: gigajoule or billion joules

MMBtu: million British thermal units

SRS: Southern Research Station of USDA Forest Service

TPO: Timber Product Output report of USDA Forest Service

Chapter 6
Economic Impact Analysis of Woody Biomass Energy Development

Alan W. Hodges

INTRODUCTION

Biomass energy facilities are often viewed in the context of local economic development efforts because utilization of biomass resources, instead of imported fossil fuels, results in greater retention of money in the local economy, leading to enhanced economic activity, income, and wealth. However, such facilities may be costly investments, on the order of tens of millions of dollars, which represents a substantial financial burden. Therefore, as a part of the public decisionmaking process, stakeholders must carefully consider overall benefits and economic impacts of such projects. Development of a biomass energy facility may have significant implications for other sectors of the local economy by posing new demands for biomass producers, equipment vendors, and other allied businesses, and with associated changes in employment and income. Economic impact analysis is a well-established methodology for evaluating the overall economic effects of an actual or proposed change in some specific activity, such as a new or expanded biomass-fueled power plant, in a local or regional economy.

Local economies may be viewed in terms of basic activities that sell goods and services to markets located outside the local area, and service activities that provide goods and services to local businesses and residents. Basic industries attract money from outside to the local economy; this money then circulates in the local area through spending and respending by service industries and by employees of businesses. Money generated by the basic industries starts a chain of spending that supports the services segment of the local economy. New dollars eventually are lost from the local economy (leakages) in the form of tax payments to State and Federal Government, savings, profits that accrue to nonresidents, and payments for goods and services imported from outside the local area. The development of biomass-fueled power plants reduces this leakage by substituting locally produced fuels for imported fuels. Also, beneficial use of waste biomass materials, such as urban tree debris and forestry residues, adds to the overall resource base.

The structure of a local economy with a biomass energy sector and the linkages that give rise to economic impacts are illustrated in **figure 6.1**. Businesses in the energy sector, including timber growers, loggers, and electric power producers, sell their products and services to intermediate and final consumers through wholesale and retail distributors, both within the local

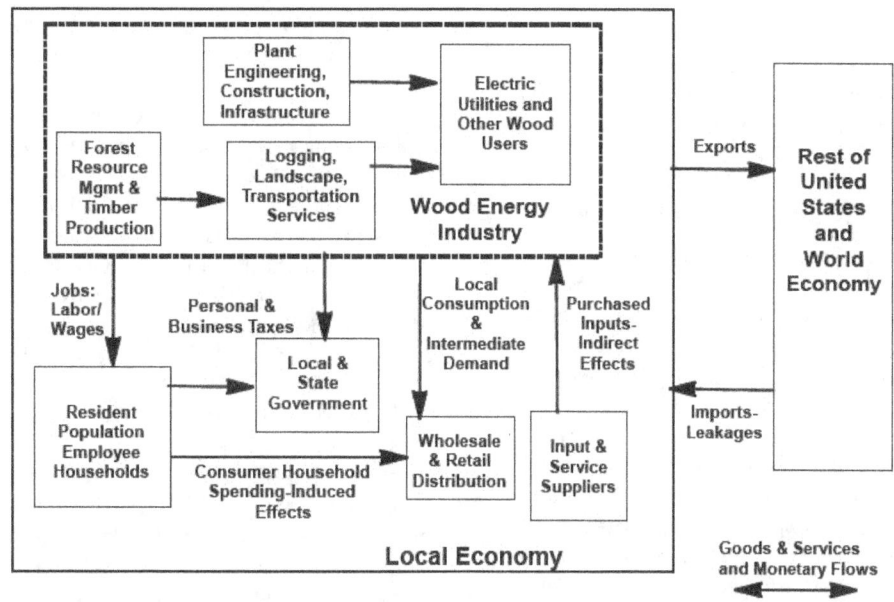

Figure 6.1—Structure and economic impacts of the wood energy industry in a local economy.

economy and to the rest of the Nation and the world. Firms that purchase inputs from local suppliers generate economic activity through recirculation of money in the local economy. Employee households spend their earnings for personal consumption of food, clothing, housing, transportation, etc., which further increases economic activity. Also, businesses and households pay taxes to local governments.

Economic impacts may be evaluated in terms of various measures that represent different aspects of economic activity. Output represents the total revenue generated by an industry, including sales, plus changes in business inventories. Employment is another important economic measure, represented simply by the number of jobs, or in some cases the number of full-time equivalents, including part-time or seasonal employees. Value added is a broad measure of income, reflecting all personal and business income, plus change in net capital investment, and is a preferred measure of net economic contribution because it avoids double counting of impacts among vertically linked sectors that may occur with output. Value added can also be construed as the difference between industry output and the value of purchases from other industry sectors, and the sum of value added for all industry sectors in a region represents the gross regional product, which is equivalent to the gross domestic product at the national level. Labor or "earned" income represents all wages and salaries and other payroll benefits paid to employees, and proprietor's income received by business owners, but excludes retirement income, welfare, and other transfer payments. Other property income includes dividends to corporate stockholders, capital gains, and interest income. Indirect business taxes represent taxes paid by businesses, such as payroll taxes, sales taxes, property taxes, and motor vehicle taxes, etc. All or some of these measures of economic impacts may be used in certain cases, depending upon the issues of concern.

Further discussion on the technical background of input-output analysis and use of the impact analyses for planning (IMPLAN) software and databases for regional economic impact analysis is provided in the appendix to this chapter.

CASE STUDIES OF WOOD-FUELED POWER PLANTS

The application of regional economic impact analysis for development of wood-fueled power plants was demonstrated through case studies of 28 selected counties in the Southern United States. The counties were identified as being favorable locations for wood-fueled power plants based on a variety of resource and socioeconomic indicators. The availability of biomass forest resources was considered for forests that do not have any administrative restrictions on commercial use, such as commercial timberlands and most national forests, but excludes parks, preserves, and wilderness areas. Data on total forest biomass, including tree tops, stumps, and small-diameter trees that would not normally be harvested for commercial timber products, were taken from the latest published inventory

estimates (Pugh 2004). Information on urban wood waste resources was compiled from various State waste management agencies, which provided this data for 7 of the 13 States. Information on population, population growth (1990–2000), personal income, income growth, and per capita income were provided by the U.S. Census Bureau (2004). Information on wildland-urban interface (WUI) areas was used as an indicator of populations that are near to biomass resources. WUI and "intermix" areas, analyzed at the census tract level, are defined as having a housing density of more than one unit per 40 acres, and located within 1.5 miles of an area of at least 1,325 acres that is 75 percent or more vegetated (Stewart and others 2005). Another factor considered was the existing output of electric power generators, as reported by U.S. Department of Energy (U.S. Department of Energy 2004).

In order to identify suitable counties for case studies of economic impacts of woody biomass power development, an index was developed. The socioeconomic and biomass resource indicators for each county were expressed as rank scores from zero to 1, with the highest value being 1 and intermediate values scaled proportionally. These variables were then combined into an overall index of suitability defined as:

$$S = FB \times (PD + PG + PIPC + PIC + WUI + E + UW)$$

where
 S = overall suitability
 FB = forest biomass per unit area
 PD = population density
 PG = population growth
 $PIPC$ = personal income per capita
 PIC = personal income change
 WUI = share of area in wildland-urban interface
 E = existing electric power generation per capita, and
 UW = urban woody waste generation per capita

The variable for forest biomass per unit area was deemed to be of critical significance, and so was specified as a multiplicative factor in this equation, while all other terms were additive. Counties were ranked according to overall scores on this suitability index, and the top-ranked five counties in each State were selected for further consideration. The final list of counties for case studies was chosen to provide a mix of different ecosystem and community types. Also, local and State officials were contacted to confirm interest and suitability of the communities identified.

The socioeconomic characteristics of the 28 selected counties are summarized in **table 6.1**, and the locations of the counties are shown on the map in **figure 6.2**. Generally, these counties were fast growing, with above-average personal income and population densities, and had a relatively high share of their area in the WUI intermix. In some States (Florida and Georgia) four or more counties were selected for case studies, while other States (Louisiana, Oklahoma, South Carolina, and Texas) had only one

Table 6.1—Socioeconomic characteristics of selected Southern U.S. counties for woody biomass power development case studies

County, State	Area	Population (2003)	Population density	Population change 1990–2000	Personal income per capita	Forest area unreserved	Share area interface	Forest biomass available	Annual woody waste per capita	Annual power generation per capita
	mile²		person per mile²	percent	dollars	acres	percent	tons per acre	tons	MWh
Lee, AL	600	119,561	199	32	21,445	393,991	46	18	NA	25
Shelby, AL	798	159,445	200	44	34,819	418,341	50	20	NA	74
Saline, AR	737	87,554	119	30	24,674	571,054	36	26	NA	0
Union, AR	1,061	44,829	42	−2	28,974	675,441	13	29	NA	58
Alachua, FL	976	223,578	229	20	25,280	604,986	43	11	0.05	8
Clay, FL	652	157,502	242	33	26,739	410,846	40	16	0.02	0
Leon, FL	704	242,577	345	32	28,056	448,549	38	16	0.13	4
Nassau, FL	612	61,625	101	31	31,298	463,899	28	18	0.03	9
Santa Rosa, FL	1,045	133,092	127	44	24,576	738,121	28	16	0.13	1
Coweta, GA	454	101,395	223	66	26,932	285,445	63	19	NA	57
Douglas, GA	200	102,015	510	30	26,085	126,809	79	27	NA	0
Murray, GA	355	39,446	111	40	20,400	214,373	40	26	NA	45
Union, GA	335	19,119	57	44	23,270	186,122	48	26	NA	1
Laurel, KY	447	55,488	124	21	20,468	282,223	56	26	0.02	2
Trimble, KY	152	8,759	58	33	17,109	99,998	45	25	0.02	498
Livingston, LA	681	102,046	150	30	21,336	449,851	53	25	NA	0
DeSoto, MS	499	124,378	249	58	27,261	317,949	19	15	0.17	5
Warren, MS	639	48,993	77	4	27,189	396,049	21	29	0.05	19
Buncombe, NC	653	212,672	326	18	27,288	416,687	72	30	0.06	10
Orange, NC	400	118,183	295	26	33,375	255,316	81	26	0.11	1
Le Flore, OK	1,639	48,896	30	11	19,776	1,007,238	6	15	NA	42
Oconee, SC	683	68,523	100	15	25,209	413,423	50	18	0.08	265
Anderson, TN	342	71,904	211	5	27,100	220,692	59	32	0.03	75
Blount, TN	569	111,510	196	23	25,353	267,666	39	24	0.04	5
Sevier, TN	605	75,503	125	39	24,603	255,145	56	27	0.06	7
Montgomery, TX	1,106	344,700	312	61	32,688	685,399	59	21	NA	5
Chesterfield, VA	437	276,840	633	24	33,586	278,264	64	25	NA	30
Fluvanna, VA	288	23,078	80	61	23,845	185,753	44	23	NA	60

NA = data not available

selected county. Forest biomass available ranged from 11 to 32 short tons per acre; county area ranged from 152 to over 1,600 square miles; populations ranged from < 10,000 to over 300,000 persons; population density ranged from 42 to 633 persons per square mile; population growth during 1990 to 2000 ranged from −2 to over 60 percent; personal income per capita ranged from about $17,000 to over $34,000; share of area in WUI ranged from 6 to 81 percent.

Costs for Power Plant Construction and Operation

Wood fuel requirements for power plants were evaluated for small and medium scales of operation, 20 and 40 MW. Energy requirements for these plants were calculated at 2.327 and 4.653 trillion British thermal units (Btus), respectively, based on plant operating rates, typical heating values for biomass, and thermal efficiency for conversion of heat energy into electric power (16,000 Btus/kW/hour), as shown in **table 6.2**. Fuel typically represents the largest operating expense for a power plant. The costs for wood

fuel to meet these energy requirements were estimated separately for each case-study county based on an analysis of wood biomass supplies of logging residues, stumps, and urban waste wood, which accounted for local collection and transportation costs (see chapter 5). Fuel costs averaged $4.0 and $9.8 million for the 20 or 40 MW plants, respectively, and ranged from $5.7 to nearly $13 million for the 40-MW plant across the selected counties, due to differences in availability of wood resources and transportation infrastructure **(table 6.3)**.

The basic information on capital expenses for power plant construction and operating expenses were provided by Carlson Consultants, a consulting engineering firm for wood-fueled power plants, as shown in **table 6.4**. Total construction costs were valued at $48.7 million for the 20-MW plant and $86.8 million for the 40-MW plant, including land, sitework, building, plant equipment, and engineering fees. The largest expense items were the boilers and turbines, at $45 to $90 million. The total

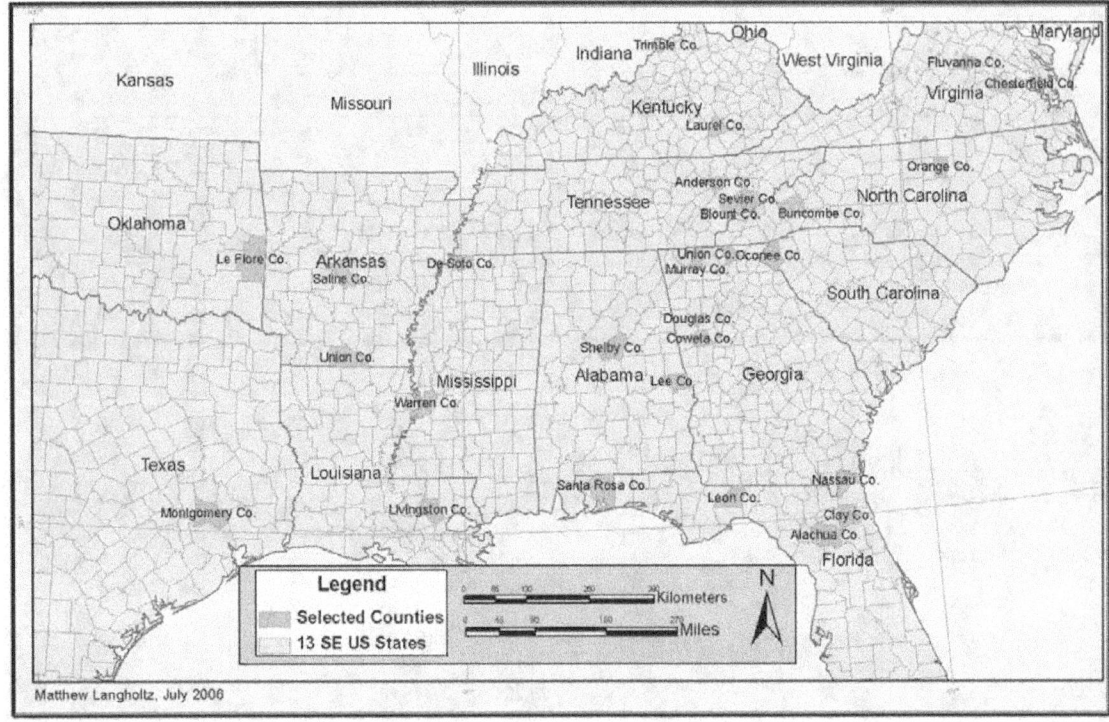

Figure 6.2—Location of counties in the Southern United States selected for case studies.

Table 6.2—Fuel requirements for a 20- and 40-MW wood-fired power plant

Factor		Datum
Total hours per year		8,760
Capacity factor		0.83
Total operating hours per year		7,271
Heat rate: Btus/kWh electricity		16,000
Total annual energy input required (trillion Btus)	**20 MW**	**2.327**
	40 MW	**4.653**

Btu = British thermal unit.
Source: Quaak and others (1999).

Table 6.3—Biomass fuel costs for 20- and 40-MW power plants in selected Southern U.S. counties

County, State	20 MW	40 MW
	million dollars	
Lee, AL	4.003	9.552
Shelby, AL	4.028	10.375
Saline, AR	4.850	11.443
Union, AR	5.021	10.912
Alachua, FL	3.840	9.278
Clay, FL	3.375	9.051
Leon, FL	4.522	10.569
Nassau, FL	3.690	9.464
Santa Rosa, FL	4.699	11.233
Coweta, GA	2.610	6.124
Douglas, GA	2.466	5.698
Murray, GA	3.702	8.697
Union, GA	4.763	11.650
Clark, KY	3.769	9.850
Laurel, KY	4.485	10.516
Trimble, KY	3.572	8.790
Livingston, LA	3.624	9.100
DeSoto, MS	3.557	9.803
Warren, MS	4.620	10.518
Orange, NC	2.880	7.375
Le Flore, OK	5.879	12.975
Buncombe, NC	3.741	9.371
Oconee, SC	4.079	10.298
Anderson, TN	4.531	11.581
Blount, TN	4.638	11.970
Sevier, TN	4.643	12.099
Montgomery, TX	2.815	6.434
Chesterfield, VA	3.811	10.224
Fluvanna, VA	4.056	10.042
Average	**4.009**	**9.827**

annual operating expenses (first year) for the model wood-fueled power plant were $8.0 million for 20 MW to $16.1 million for 40 MW, including average fuel costs as discussed above. In terms of the earlier discussion, these values reflect the direct effect of the new facility. The construction expenditures are a one-time event that was assumed to occur within a year, while plant operating expenditures are annually recurring impacts. It was assumed that all purchases were made locally, except in some cases where particular inputs may not be available locally because the producing sector does not exist in the county.

Economic Impact Results

The economic impacts of a 20- and 40-MW wood-fueled power plant were evaluated in each of the case-study communities (counties) using the IMPLAN software and regional databases (see appendix for details).

The estimated economic impacts resulting from the construction phase of power plant development in each of the counties are summarized in **table 6.5**. Total output impacts for a 20-MW power plant averaged $11.9 million and ranged from $2.8 to $45.3

Table 6.4—Capital and operating costs for a 20- and 40-MW wood-fueled power plant

IMPLAN sector(s)	Description	20 MW	40 MW
		$1000	
	Capital construction costs		
39	Site preparation (highway, street)	800	1,000
40	Water, sewer, and pipeline construction	100	150
238	Power boiler and heat exchanger manufacturing	22,250	40,500
285	Turbine and turbine generator set units manufacturing	22,250	40,500
394	Initial fuel delivery (truck transportation)	300	500
429	Financing cost (funds, trusts, and other financial vehicles)	1,500	2,500
431	Site acquisition (real estate)	1,000	1,000
445	Permitting (environmental and other technical consulting)	500	600
	Total	**48,700**	**86,750**
	Annual operating costs (1st year)		
14–18	Wood fuel cost, average for all counties (allocated equally to logging, agriculture, and forestry support services)	4,009	9,827
30	Utility interconnection (power generation and supply)	100	155
31	Start-up fuel, gas (natural gas distribution)	25	50
32	Utilities, electric	50	75
150	Consumable chemicals	330	660
238	Power boiler and heat exchanger manufacturing	50	90
285	Turbine and turbine generator set units manufacturing	50	90
428	Insurance (insurance agencies, brokerages, and related)	160	260
434	Mobil equipment lease	90	120
439	Routine and periodic maintenance	1,000	1,650
445	Environmental costs	100	160
451	Corporate overhead (management)	100	120
452	Office expenses	110	140
460	Ash disposal	60	120
499	Property tax	470	800
10006	Salaries and benefits	1,260	1,820
	Total	**7,964**	**16,137**

IMPLAN = impact analyses for planning.
Source: Carlson Small Power Consultants, Redding, CA.

Table 6.5—Capital construction impacts for 20- and 40-MW wood-fueled power plants in selected Southern U.S. counties

County, State	20-MW plant			40-MW plant		
	Output	Employment	Value added	Output	Employment	Value added
	million $	*no. jobs*	*- - - - - - million $ - - - - -*		*no. jobs*	*million $*
Lee, AL	5.0	60	2.9	6.0	72	3.4
Shelby, AL	40.9	317	18.9	71.2	549	32.5
Saline, AR	4.1	52	2.3	4.9	61	2.7
Union, AR	4.0	46	2.3	4.8	55	2.7
Alachua, FL	8.0	81	4.3	10.8	107	10.8
Clay, FL	7.6	74	3.7	10.3	98	4.8
Leon, FL	7.8	74	4.1	10.7	100	5.4
Nassau, FL	6.7	63	3.3	9.0	82	4.2
Santa Rosa, FL	37.7	335	15.4	65.5	578	26.3
Coweta, GA	7.5	49	2.7	5.6	59	3.1
Douglas, GA	7.6	69	3.6	10.2	90	4.6
Murray, GA	3.1	31	1.7	3.8	39	2.0
Union, GA	4.0	47	2.2	4.8	57	2.6
Laurel, KY	4.5	54	2.6	5.4	64	3.1
Trimble, KY	2.8	27	1.7	4.6	43	2.7
Livingstone, LA	35.0	293	17.2	61.2	504	29.9
DeSoto, MS	4.8	59	2.7	5.8	70	3.1
Warren, MS	4.4	54	2.4	5.2	64	2.8
Buncombe, NC	7.9	74	3.9	10.7	98	10.7
Orange, NC	45.3	379	25.9	78.7	653	44.9
Le Flore, OK	5.8	65	2.5	7.8	83	3.0
Oconee, SC	4.2	45	2.4	5.0	54	2.8
Anderson, TN	6.7	57	3.6	9.1	76	4.7
Blount, TN	4.9	48	3.0	5.9	58	3.6
Sevier, TN	6.7	59	3.5	11.5	229	7.0
Montgomery, TX	7.8	64	4.1	10.6	85	5.4
Chesterfield, VA	43.8	222	22.1	76.2	372	38.2
Fluvanna, VA	3.9	40	2.1	4.7	50	2.5
Average	**11.9**	**101**	**6.0**	**18.6**	**159**	**9.6**

million; employment impacts averaged 103 jobs and ranged from 31 to 379 jobs; value added impacts averaged $6.0 million and ranged from $1.5 to $25.9 million. For a 40-MW power plant, output impacts of capital construction averaged $18.5 million and ranged from $3.4 to $78.7 million; employment impacts averaged 159 jobs and ranged from 39 to 653 jobs; value added impacts averaged $9.2 million and ranged from $1.8 to $44.9 million. The large range of values is due to the fact that some counties have local sources for purchase of the major capital items, while in other cases these items must be imported from other regions, which represents a leakage from the local economy.

The economic impacts of annual operations in the first year for power plants in each county are summarized in **table 6.6**. Total output impacts for a 20-MW plant averaged $10.6 million and ranged from $2.8 to $14.4 million; employment impacts averaged 170 jobs and ranged from 27 to 266 jobs; value added impacts averaged $6.3 million and ranged from $1.7 to $8.6 million. For the 40-MW plant, total output impacts of operations averaged $21.7 million and ranged from $4.6 to $31.5 million; employment impacts averaged 370 jobs and ranged from 43 to 629 jobs; value added impacts averaged $13.0 million and ranged from $2.8 to $18.9 million. These results for plant operations can be

Table 6.6—Annual operating impacts (1st year) for 20- and 40-MW wood-fueled power plants in selected Southern U.S. counties

County, State	20-MW plant			40-MW plant		
	Output	Employment	Value added	Output	Employment	Value added
	million $	*no. jobs*	*- - - - million $ - - - - -*		*no. jobs*	*million $*
Lee, AL	12.40	210	7.63	25.25	447	15.69
Shelby, AL	11.35	125	7.28	24.33	276	15.76
Saline, AR	11.75	239	6.98	24.24	522	14.47
Union, AR	12.84	226	7.39	25.18	461	14.51
Alachua, FL	13.52	196	8.38	27.54	413	17.08
Clay, FL	11.73	182	7.10	25.30	420	15.35
Leon, FL	13.41	156	8.55	27.14	318	17.35
Nassau, FL	10.80	137	6.71	23.06	297	14.56
Santa Rosa, FL	12.47	147	7.70	25.94	307	16.18
Coweta, GA	9.51	160	5.52	18.41	331	10.71
Douglas, GA	7.96	75	4.46	14.21	130	7.84
Murray, GA	6.22	54	3.09	11.99	100	5.73
Union, GA	11.28	214	6.81	24.34	482	14.82
Laurel, KY	12.33	240	7.02	25.23	519	14.34
Trimble, KY	2.83	27	1.71	4.57	43	2.75
Livingston, LA	9.64	158	5.73	20.38	349	12.19
DeSoto, MS	8.27	155	5.18	16.70	356	10.83
Warren, MS	11.87	182	7.12	23.74	375	14.30
Buncombe, NC	12.84	242	7.59	26.65	546	15.77
Orange, NC	10.81	177	6.91	22.08	393	14.07
Le Flore, OK	8.22	85	3.88	15.78	155	7.38
Oconee, SC	10.76	220	5.98	23.16	508	12.86
Anderson, TN	11.51	216	6.94	24.96	510	15.08
Blount, TN	14.40	266	8.63	31.48	629	18.91
Sevier, TN	8.90	216	5.65	18.24	509	11.94
Montgomery, TX	11.32	154	6.79	21.73	314	13.03
Chesterfield, VA	13.08	187	7.84	28.46	437	17.07
Fluvanna, VA	9.56	218	5.51	20.42	501	11.89
Average	**10.57**	**169.61**	**6.31**	**21.67**	**370.12**	**13.00**

considered as "permanent" impacts over the life of the plant. Again, the operating impacts varied widely among counties due to differences in the specific makeup of the local (county) economy, and in some cases, the absence of key sectors serving wood-fired power plant operations. If we consider the average of total output impacts for a 40-MW plant ($21.7 million) in comparison to the average direct expense for operations ($16.1 million), it would appear that there is an implicit multiplier effect of 1.35. In other words, the total impacts were 1.35 times the original expenditure. It was assumed in this analysis that the development of a wood-fueled power plant would utilize the existing infrastructure for power distribution.

Often it is important to understand the distribution of economic impacts across various sectors of the local economy. The estimated employment impacts of annual operations for a 40-MW power plant in each county are shown by major industry group in **table 6.7**, according to the North American Industry Classification System. A large employment impact, averaging 226 jobs, or 61 percent of total impacts, occurred in the agriculture and forestry sector, which supplies wood fuel to these plants, while there were also significant employment impacts in the sectors for professional services (27 jobs), retail trade (19 jobs), and government (22 jobs), reflecting the indirect and induced effects on the local economy.

Table 6.7—Average employment impacts by industry group for annual operations (1st year) of 40-MW wood-fueled power plants in selected Southern U.S. counties

Industry group[a]	Average number jobs	Percent of total jobs
11 Agriculture, Forestry, Fishing and Hunting	226	61.2
21 Mining	0	0.0
22 Utilities	1	0.4
23 Construction	8	2.1
31–33 Manufacturing	2	0.6
42 Wholesale Trade	3	0.9
44–45 Retail Trade	19	5.2
48–49 Transportation and Warehousing	2	0.6
51 Information	1	0.3
52 Finance and Insurance	7	1.9
53 Real Estate and Rental and Leasing	5	1.4
54 Professional, Scientific and Technical Services	27	7.2
55 Management of Companies and Enterprises	1	0.4
56 Administrative and Support and Waste Management and Remediation Services	7	1.9
61 Educational Services	1	0.3
62 Health Care and Social Assistance	12	3.1
71 Arts, Entertainment, and Recreation	2	0.5
72 Accommodation and Food Services	12	3.2
81 Other Services (except Public Administration)	9	2.6
92 Public Administration	22	6.0
Total	**370**	**100.0**

[a] North American Industry Classification System

CONCLUSIONS

Potential economic impacts of wood-fueled power plants were examined for 28 counties in the Southern United States that were identified as highly suitable based on socioeconomic criteria. Construction and ongoing operations of wood-fueled power plants may have significant local economic impacts, but these impacts varied widely among selected counties, depending upon the particular makeup of the local economy. Utilization of wood fuel represents one of the largest expenditures for a power plant, and gives rise to large impacts in the local forestry and forestry services sectors. Other sectors of the local economy are also impacted through the indirect and induced effects of supply chain purchases and employee spending. Impacts of a 40-MW power plant are greater than for a 20-MW plant, although not in proportion to the power output, due to economies of scale. More precise estimates of economic impacts may be gained through site-specific engineering studies and customized regional input-output models.

REFERENCES

Johnson, K.P.; Kort, J.R. 2004. Redefinition of the BEA economic areas. Survey of Current Business. Nov.: 68–75.

Miller, R.E.; Blair, P.D. 1985. Input-output analysis: foundations and extensions. Englewood Cliffs, NJ: Prentice-Hall. 464 p.

Minnesota IMPLAN Group (MIG), Inc. 1999. IMPLAN pro user's guide, analysis guide, data guide. Version 2.0. Stillwater, MN: Minnesota Implan Group, Inc. 418 p. [Current pricing for IMPLAN regional data and other background information available at http://www.implan.com.]

Pugh, Scott A. 2004. RPA data wiz users guide. Version 1.0. GTR–NC–242. St. Paul, MN: U.S. Department of Agriculture Forest Service, North Central Research Station. 135 p.

Quaak, P.; Knoef, H.; Stassen, H. 1999. Energy from biomass: a review of combustion and gasification technologies. World Bank Tech. Pap. 422. Energy series. World Bank, NY. 99 p.

Stewart, S.; Radeloff, V.; Hammer, R. [and others]. 2005. Mapping the wildland urban interface and projecting its growth to 2030. Misc. publication. Evanston, IL: U.S. Department of Agriculture Forest Service, North Central Research Station. 38 p.

U.S. Department of Commerce, Bureau of Economic Analysis. 2004. Personal income statistics for United States counties. http://www.bea.doc.gov. [Date accessed: March 8, 2005].

U.S. Department of Commerce, Census Bureau. 2004. Annual benchmark report for retail trade and food services: January 1992 through February 2004. Current Bus. Rep. BR/03–A. Washington, DC. 98 p.

U.S. Department of Commerce, Census Bureau. 2004. Estimates of current population for U.S. counties. http://www.census.gov/popest/estimates.php. [Date accessed: March 8, 2005].

U.S. Department of Energy, Energy Information Administration. 2004. U.S. electric generation. EIA 860 and EIA–906/920 Rep. Washington, DC. [Not paged].

Appendix: Input-Output Analysis and IMPLAN Software/Databases for Economic Impact Analysis

INPUT-OUTPUT ANALYSIS

Economic impact analysis is typically done using an analytical procedure known as input-output (I–O) analysis, which quantifies the structural relationships and interactions between industry sectors, households, and governments within a local economy (Miller and Blair 1985). I–O models are constructed from a transactions table that reflects the value of goods and services exchanged between all sectors of the economy in a 1-year base period.

A simple example of a transactions table for a local economy is shown in **table A.6.1** for an economy with four major industry sectors (agriculture, manufacturing, mining, and trade). In this example, the agricultural sector has total output of 39 units, of which 30 are sold to other producing industries as intermediate inputs, including 12 to other components of the agricultural sector, 2 to mining, 10 to manufacturing, and 6 to trade, then the remaining 9 are sold to final consumers. To produce its output, the agricultural sector makes purchases from other parts of the agricultural sector (12) and from each of the other producing industries, including 5 from mining, 5 from manufacturing, 2 from trade, and 7 from services, and 8 are value added inputs for profits, indirect business taxes, and payments to households.

Changes in final demand, including local consumption and exports cause producing industries to respond accordingly to meet this change in demand. The value added section of the transaction table shows how each sector is linked to household income in the local area, and the household component of final demand reflect how each sector is impacted by local household spending. Producing industries in the economy are each listed twice in the transactions table, as both sellers and buyers of commodities. Rows in the table reflect the sales of output by each producing industry, including intermediate sales to other industries or institutions, and to final consumers such as households, government, and exports. Columns in the table reflect purchases by each producing industry from other industries, as well as value added inputs for payments to workers, taxes, owner profits, and imports. The table is balanced such that the total output of each producing industry equals the total value of purchases by that industry. Values are expressed in dollars or millions of dollars. In some formulations of I–O models, households may be shown as a producing industry that sells services (labor) and purchases inputs (consumption) in order to capture the effects of spending associated with changes in household earnings. An elaboration of the I–O model, known as social accounting matrices (SAM), enables the model to capture the effects of inventory change, capital investments, and transfer payments for nonearned income such as pensions and welfare.

The linkages inherent in an I–O or SAM model are represented by economic multipliers that measure the total impact of a change in one or more industries on all other industries within the local economy (Miller and Blair 1985). Multipliers are derived from the transactions table using matrix mathematical procedures. An increase or decrease in output or employment within a specified

Table A.6.1—An example transactions table for an input-output model of a local economy

Selling industries	Purchasing industries					Final demand			Total
	Agriculture	Mining	Manufacturing	Trade	Services	Households	Government	Exports	
Agriculture	12	2	10	6	0	1	1	7	**39**
Mining	5	2	20	0	0	0	2	11	**40**
Manufacturing	5	3	6	20	5	9	10	40	**98**
Trade	2	3	2	1	5	25	10	5	**53**
Services	7	10	30	2	10	18	10	0	**87**
Value added									
Labor earnings	5	14	20	12	35				**75**
Profits	1	2	3	4	10				**20**
Imports	1	2	3	4	22				**32**
Total	**39**	**40**	**98**	**53**	**87**	**53**	**33**	**63**	**684**

Note: value added components do not apply to final demand.

industry is said to have a "multiplier effect" in the local economy. For a given industry, the size of the multiplier depends on the size of the economy and the degree of economic integration among regional businesses, and the level of sales outside the local region or exports. Firms that purchase more local inputs have higher multipliers as do firms with greater external sales. For each industry, multipliers estimate three components of total change within the local area: direct, indirect, and induced effects. Direct effects represent the initial change in the industry in question. Indirect effects represent changes in interindustry transactions as supplying industries respond to changes in demands from the directly affected industries. Induced effects reflect changes in local spending that result from income changes in the directly and indirectly affected industry sectors. Total effects multipliers usually range from 1.5 to 2.5, meaning that there will be a total change of 1.5 to 2.5 times the original direct change. IMPLAN multipliers are available for all of the basic impact measures, including output, employment, value added, labor income, employee compensation, other property income, and indirect business taxes. Output multipliers relate the changes in sales to final demand by one industry to total changes in output (gross sales) by all industries within the local area. Income multipliers relate the change in direct income to changes in total income or to changes in output within the local economy. Employment multipliers relate changes in direct employment or output to total employment effects, and may be stated either as a ratio of total to direct employment, or as a number of jobs per million dollars of output change. Value added multipliers are interpreted the same as income and employment multipliers; they relate changes in value added in the industry experiencing the direct effect to total changes in value added for the entire local economy.

I–O and SAM models have a number of standard assumptions and limitations that should be recognized. These models are fixed in their parameters, with constant technical relationships between industry sectors and constant prices or relationships between quantity and value. This means that changes in market prices and substitution of inputs or technologies are not allowed. Also, there are no capacity constraints to any shocks imposed to the system, so very large changes can lead to estimated impacts that unrealistically exceed local industry capacity.

IMPLAN SOFTWARE AND DATABASES

IMPLAN is a proprietary computer software package and associated databases that enable the construction of regional I–O models for any area of the United States. IMPLAN is an acronym for impact analyses for planning. The computer program was originally developed by the Forest Service in cooperation with the Federal Emergency Management Agency and the U.S. Department of the Interior, Bureau of Land Management, to assist in land and resource management planning. Since 1993, the IMPLAN system has been developed under exclusive rights by the Minnesota

IMPLAN Group, Inc., which licenses and distributes the software to users. IMPLAN has become the standard tool of economic impact analysis in the United States, with hundreds of licensed users, including universities, government agencies, and private companies.

The economic data for IMPLAN is based on the system of national accounts for the United States, including information collected by the U.S. Department of Commerce, the U.S. Bureau of Labor Statistics, and other Federal and State Government Agencies. Data are compiled for 509 distinct producing industry sectors of the national economy defined according the North American Industrial Classification System (NAICS) based upon the primary commodity or service produced. Since 2001, the NAICS has supplanted the previous Standard Industrial Classification system in order to harmonize the economic statistics for the United States, Canada, and Mexico, as required under the North American Free Trade Agreement. Industry data incorporated in the model includes output, value added, employment, wages and business taxes paid, inputs purchased from other sectors, imports and exports, final demand by households and government, capital investment, business inventories, marketing margins, and inflation factors (deflators). The technological relationships between industry sectors reflect the benchmark I–O tables of the national economy, which are updated every 5 years based on the economic census conducted by the U.S. Census Bureau. State and county-level data on employment, income, and population are the basis for IMPLAN I–O tables for local areas. Regional datasets for IMPLAN are updated annually for all counties in the United States. These data enable construction of I–O models for individual counties or for larger geographic areas such as clusters of contiguous counties or States. The regional datasets are purchased separately. IMPLAN software, data, and training are relatively inexpensive, making this system affordable for most organizations. Further technical details are provided in the IMPLAN User's Guide (Minnesota IMPLAN Group, Inc. 1999) and Web site (www.implan.com).

Economic impact analysis with the IMPLAN software is conducted by specifying changes in the value of output or employment for particular sectors. Output and employment are interchangeable, and a change in one measure implies a change in the other according to the output per employee ratio. It does not matter whether the change is positive or negative; in either case the same multipliers are invoked. Values in IMPLAN may have a specified percentage of the expenditure that applies locally, or optionally, the local share may correspond to the regional purchase coefficient for the given industry sector, which represents the average share of inputs of a given commodity that are purchased from local sources. Any share < 100 percent means that the impact will be reduced because a portion of the value is lost as a "leakage" from the local economy.

Values for commodities in IMPLAN are stated in producer prices, i.e., the prices of goods at the factory or production point. For manufactured goods, the price paid by final consumers equals the producer price plus margins that accrue to the wholesale, retail, and transportation sectors. IMPLAN contains information on typical margins for many different sectors, which may be optionally used to more accurately capture the effects of marketing chains. For service businesses, such as restaurants or hotels, the producer and purchaser prices are equivalent. For impact analysis of retail businesses, it is important to include only the gross margin on sales as a measure of output change, since most manufacture goods purchased at retail by consumers are produced outside the local area. Typical gross margins are available for broad types of retail establishments from the U.S. Census Bureau.

IMPLAN models are constructed for a specific base year. Impact events specified for any other year must be deflated to express in model-year monetary terms, in order to maintain the proper relationships between employment and output values. The software contains deflator factors for each specific industry and year, which are automatically applied when impact events are specified. By default, impact analysis results are given in the model-year dollars, however, results may be reported in deflated terms for any particular year.

IMPLAN models may be extensively modified and customized to take advantage of more specific information available about the study region or particular industries being examined. When used with all parameters set at default levels, IMPLAN models reflect prevailing national technical relationships and regional industry activity. In some cases, however, a particular industry may not be well represented by the national average technical coefficients. Some of the model information that an analyst may wish to modify includes industry output or employment, trade flows, commodity demand, industry production functions, or byproducts. For example, electric power plants that utilize wood fuels may differ significantly from the electric power industry at large. Also, one or two new industry sectors may be created to represent activities that are not well represented by any of the standard industry sectors.

I–O models are constructed for an explicitly defined geographic area, so the definition of the region can be an important issue that may dramatically affect the results. IMPLAN offers flexibility to create regional economic models for individual counties, groups of counties, or States, depending upon the nature of the activity being evaluated. In general, the region should be defined large enough to encompass all of the local employment activity related to the affected industries. Typically, the region for impact analysis within a small- to medium-sized municipality would be the surrounding county, whereas an analysis of a large city or metro area would probably include a group of several counties. Also, the particular location of a facility may affect the definition of an appropriate regional model. For example, if a new plant is to be located near a county boundary, the neighboring county should probably be included in the regional model since it will be influenced by the facility. In cases where there is no compelling logical basis for definition of the region, the functional economic areas defined by the U.S. Department of Commerce, Bureau of Economic Analysis represent natural regions for economic impact analysis, which are based on analysis of worker commuting patterns reported in the decennial census of population and housing, together with other information such as newspaper readership (Johnson and Kort 2004).

Chapter 7
Public Perceptions of Using Wood for Fuel

Martha C. Monroe, Richard Plate, Lauren McDonell, and Annie Oxarart

INTRODUCTION

Using wood from the wildland-urban interface (WUI) for fuel is advantageous because the close proximity of the forest to the facility reduces transportation costs for potential power users. In areas of rapid interface development, waste wood from land clearing can be a significant, though unsustainable, source of fuel. In areas of active forest management and extensive urban forests, sustainable sources of wood are available (see Langholtz and others, this publication). With careful planning and effective management, placing a woody biomass facility in the interface can be a reasonable decision. While there are significant concerns associated with using woody biomass, the planning process can be severely compromised if the public is not aware of the advantages and disadvantages of this resource. In the case of large-scale energy facilities or public utilities, local residents may expect to be involved in discussions about facility design. A number of studies (Upreti 2004, van der Hoorst 2002) cite public perception as playing a pivotal role in the success or failure of proposed biomass energy plants. Projects can stall, funds can be denied, and lawsuits can spell doom if the public does not support an initiative. With public support, however, projects can move forward in a spirit of cooperation and exploration.

The likelihood and level of public support for utilizing woody biomass may be difficult to predict because support varies widely in the context of various biomass fuels and the preferences people have for management of nearby forests. The characteristics that affect proposals for using woody biomass for energy can be divided into three categories: perceptions of biomass in general, perceptions of forest sustainability, and perceptions of risk. The first three sections of this chapter review and interpret the available literature in the context of these three categories. The fourth section reports efforts to understand the public perceptions of using woody biomass in Gainesville, FL, where a pilot study of the Wood to Energy Outreach Program has been underway.

PUBLIC PERCEPTIONS OF BIOMASS

According to a series of polls conducted by utility companies across the United States from 1995 to 1997, residential customers favored renewable sources of electricity, with the majority of these customers stating a willingness to pay more per month on their electric bills for power generated from a renewable source (Bang and others 2000, Farhar 1999).

Such news bodes well for proponents of biomass energy, except that respondents probably were not thinking about biomass when they completed the poll. These customers generally received the idea of biomass with less enthusiasm than other renewable energy sources like solar and wind. For example, when customers were asked about their preferred renewable energy options, solar, wind, and geothermal all received approval ratings above 60 percent, while biomass was much lower at 32 percent. Furthermore, more respondents (45 percent) were unwilling to bear additional costs associated with electricity produced from biomass than for wind (31 percent) or solar (35 percent). While a majority (53 percent) expressed a willingness to pay at least $4 more per month for biomass energy, this response is markedly lower than for other alternative energy sources (Farhar 1999). It is difficult to know if respondents are particularly displeased about utilizing biomass or are merely uninformed about this energy source.

Upreti (2004) attributes results like those reported by Farhar to a perceived advantage of energy sources that do not emit any pollutants, such as solar and wind, over those sources that are renewable but require a smokestack. Like conventional fuels, biomass energy involves combustion and, thus, prompts the perception that it creates air pollution. Consequently, it is deemed less attractive than other renewable energy sources. This might also explain the relative advantage that natural gas enjoys over other combustible energy sources—an energy source widely acclaimed to be "clean" is perceived to create no air pollution (Farhar 1999).

The concern over emissions is also apparent when analyzing perceptions of those who reside near a proposed facility. Key concerns from those residing near proposed facility sites included potential risk to health and safety, ecological concerns, potential for increased traffic, and the visual intrusion of the structure on the previously rural landscape (Upreti 2004). Some of these concerns are only relevant to facilities sited in rural areas and would not be as relevant to facilities in the WUI. These perceptions and concerns parallel those associated with other industrial developments that pose potential hazards (Khan 2004, Rosch and Kaltschmitt 1999). Perceived health risks also depend upon the fuel being burned (van den Hoogen and others 2002). Fuels perceived as dirty, e.g., chicken manure or sewer sludge, evoke much stronger concerns than do fuels perceived as cleaner, such as wood. Perceptions of the economic benefits of a biomass facility—primarily in the form of new jobs—may or may not be sufficient to sway local residents to favor such facilities; how people perceive the benefits depends on some of the other variables discussed throughout this review (Rosch and Kaltschmitt 1999, van der Horst 2005).

Questions about the viability of using biomass are not limited to neighbors of bioenergy facilities. A number of environmental organizations have expressed similar concerns. While the U.S. Department of Energy, National Renewable Energy Laboratory regards biomass as an important tool for controlling greenhouse gas emissions and dependence on foreign oil (National Renewable Energy Laboratory 2009), environmental organizations are more wary of the potential problems of burning biomass. For example, the Natural Resource Defense Council (NRDC) views biomass as a beneficial fuel source that is renewable and can generate rural job opportunities, farmer revenue, and highly skilled positions, yet NRDC is concerned about the sustainability of the sources of wood and overall air quality, particularly for home heating (Natural Resource Defense Council 2003).

One significant challenge to engaging the public in discussions about using wood for energy is that Americans know very little about energy in general. According to a 2002 national survey (National Environmental Education and Training Foundation 2002), only 12 percent of Americans can pass a basic quiz on energy knowledge. In addition, Americans overestimate their knowledge, believing that they have a lot or a fair amount of knowledge about energy. Misconceptions abound about the average gas mileage achieved by American vehicles, the causes of electricity shortages, the availability of new sources of energy, the sources of current energy, and nuclear waste storage (National Environmental Education and Training Foundation 2002). The lack of knowledge about basic energy issues makes it difficult for the American public to discuss options, learn about choices, and make good decisions about energy consumption and conservation, effectively maintaining our reliance on imported and domestic fossil fuels (National Environmental Education and Training Foundation 2002). One explanation for this energy illiteracy is our unfamiliarity with energy resources—our system provides relatively cheap electricity from distant sources with the flick of a switch.

Knowledge about woody biomass energy is also lacking. For example, a mail survey of five counties in Florida revealed that 94 percent of the respondents were familiar with the issue of global warming, but over 55 percent were unfamiliar with biomass as a source of energy and 68 percent had not heard of cofiring (Adams 2003). Despite this lack of knowledge, they were willing to pay $5 to $20 more on each utility bill for cleaner energy technology that would reduce the effects of global warming. However, this willingness to contribute to cleaner energy does not translate into action. Over 50 percent of the respondents were not aware their utility provided such programs and < 6 percent were currently subscribed to them (Adams 2003).

Even in Europe, where a number of biomass facilities are in operation, public awareness of the benefits from biomass is rather low and less is known about it than other forms of renewable energy (Rohracher and others 2004). Lack of knowledge in Europe, however, may not translate into a negative image about its use. Surveys in Austria show that attitudes toward biomass depend on who is promoting it, previous experience, and local politics (Rohracher and others 2004).

In general, the public does not perceive biomass to have the positive characteristics associated with noncombustible forms of renewable energy, and the public is concerned about impacts on air quality, health, traffic, and the environment. There is little evidence that woody biomass is perceived any differently. This literature review summarizes the general concerns associated with converting any biomass to energy, i.e., combustion or gasification. However, concerns about using woody biomass extend beyond the facility operations to the forests that are the source. The following section looks specifically at concerns regarding the sustainable management of woody biomass sources.

PUBLIC PERCEPTIONS OF FOREST SUSTAINABILITY

Some woody biomass proposals have been rejected by local residents because of perceived negative environmental impacts (Upreti 2004). One factor that undermines citizen approval of using wood for energy is the perception that forests will be poorly managed or destroyed to supply the necessary quantity of fuel. Several national environmental advocacy groups, e.g., Natural Resource Defense Council (2003) and Greenpeace (2005), express support for biomass energy but emphasize that such support is contingent upon the availability of forests that are managed sustainably. Within some organizations, however, local opinions do not follow national policy. For example, the local conservation chair of the Suwannee-St. Johns Sierra Club promotes the use of woody biomass from all sustainably managed forests (Dickinson 2005), even though the official national Sierra Club position opposes harvesting federally owned forests for electricity generation (Sierra Club 2007). One way to mitigate concerns about forest sustainability may be through forest certification systems that establish criteria for sustainable forest management.

Concerns about forest management and the tendency to value preserved forests more than working forests may be an outgrowth of demographic change across the South. The South's population is growing rapidly—over 11 million people were added (representing 11.5-percent growth) between 2000 and 2008 (U.S. Department of Commerce 2008). In addition, the South has been growing faster than other regions of the Nation, recording both the largest increase and the fastest growth rate between 2004 and 2005 (U.S. Department of Commerce 2005). Some migrants from other regions of the country have brought wealth and a diversity of experience to their new communities in the South (Tarrant and others 2002). Urbanization has changed the way residents know and use nearby forests.

A telephone survey of 7,000 Americans suggests that the public supports ecosystem health, protecting watersheds, and nonconsumptive uses of national forests (Shields 2002). Policies that restrict timber and mineral extraction and support ecosystem protection are favored more by residents of the Eastern United States and metropolitan residents of the Western United States than by residents of nonmetropolitan Western States (Shields 2002).This demonstrates that the trend toward ecosystem protection and away from timber production is also echoed in the South.

In a 2001 telephone survey of 1,423 urban and rural residents of the 13 Southern States, the majority of respondents said that they believed the most important value of forests was clean air and the least important was wood production (Tarrant and others 2002). Respondents favored government funding for environmental protection and stricter environmental regulations, but did not extend these preservationist values to private forests (Tarrant and others 2002).

Over the last 20 years, attitudes toward forest management have moved away from traditional timber production and toward protection, which could be a consequence of changing demographics, increased economic growth, greater technological innovations (Tarrant and others 2002), or a perceived scarcity of the resource.

But in the South, unlike the West, the majority of forest land is privately owned—in some States, total private ownership is as high as 95 percent and nonindustrial private forest (NIPF) owners account for as much as 77 percent (U.S. Department of Agriculture 2004). If NIPF landowners are interested in the potential financial gain that new markets associated with an increase in woody biomass would bring, they could help sway public opinion to support using woody biomass. But because NIPF landowner attitudes in some areas of the South are indistinguishable from their urban counterparts, these landowners may not be interested in marketing biomass for energy (Bliss and others 1997, Tarrant and others 2002). Most NIPF landowners currently manage their forests for both economic and noneconomic nontimber objectives (Bourke and Luloff 1994, Sinclair and Knuth 2000). Nevertheless, in WUI areas where the public wishes to maintain forest cover and direct development, it may be possible to obtain NIPF landowner support and approval for a woody biomass proposal that sustains private forests. Working with NIPF landowners may be an important element of a community woody biomass plan.

In Finland, where the majority (62 percent) of forest land ownership is NIPF, results of a mail survey suggested that these landowners have positive attitudes about using wood for energy production. They felt that using wood for energy positively influenced the forest ecosystem, climate, employment, economic activity in rural areas, and recreational opportunities (Toivonen and others 2002). Of those who harvested wood for energy, over

three-fourths of the respondents said they do so to improve the management of young stands, to enhance reforestation efforts, and to fuel their own homes. Those owners who did not harvest their forests were generally urban dwellers.

In WUI areas, rural farms and working private forests are being converted into subdivisions and private parks. Residents of these areas may not perceive nearby green spaces as a resource that can be sustainably harvested, utilized, and renewed. New residents in the South may not be aware that pulp plantations have short rotations and, although recently harvested areas can look barren and bleak, they can become covered with vigorous green saplings in as little as 3 years from harvest. A new resident's initial opposition to timber harvesting will likely need to be met with significant educational efforts explaining the benefits and operations of basic, sustainable forest management and the costs and benefits of using wood for energy.

PERCEPTIONS OF RISK

Few studies have been conducted specifically on public perceptions of woody biomass, so we have gathered information about other types of biomass and other types of incinerators to describe how the public might respond to woody biomass proposals. The level of trust citizens have in the development and management of any proposed industrial facility is very important, and biomass energy plants are no exception (Sinclair and Lofstedt 2001). For example, public trust in the facility owner and operator has been cited as a central factor in the acceptance of a biomass energy plant (Rosch and Kaltschmitt 1999). Failure of plant proposals in the United Kingdom has been attributed to questions about the validity of environmental impact statements made by developers in their planning applications (van der Hoorst and others 2002). Several types of trust are involved—a broad trust in the government or other large institutions and more specific trust in a particular developer or manager (Ibiatayo and Pijawka 1999). A developer who is able to gain citizens' trust on a personal level can overcome broad distrust in government and institutions. In some cases, partnerships involving government ownership combined with operation by a private company can serve to increase public trust in the operation as a whole (Ibiatayo 2002).

Research in this area is often approached in the context of risk communication, which emphasizes the need to engage the public in a dialogue aimed at understanding and addressing concerns. Establishing trust requires including the public early in the planning process for a proposed facility (Ibiatayo and Pijawka 1999, Kunreuther and others 1996, Rabe 1994, van der Horst and others 2002). Typically, the public is included only after a controversy has arisen, resulting in low levels of trust before the dialogue has even begun (Lofstedt 1999). When public involvement begins early in the planning process, as was the case in planning a hazardous waste facility in Alberta, Canada, the perceptions of the potential risks might be greatly reduced (Baxter and Greenlaw 2005). The perception of being "competent, open, fair, concerned and reliable" can be established in the beginning and is vital to achieving and maintaining a high level of public trust throughout the process of establishing a facility (Lofstedt 1999).

Preexisting ideological beliefs are also key factors in the perception of a proposed facility. For example, residents of four towns involved in the process to site the Alberta hazardous waste facility varied in their perceptions of risk; their variations stemmed from different levels of comfort with uncertainty, identification of their communities as being primarily rural or urban, and feelings about being treated fairly (Baxter and Greenlaw 2005).

Whether community members perceive their community as part of an expanding urban system or as an independent rural entity may be particularly important when siting a facility in the WUI. For example, residents of Barrhead in Alberta, Canada, a community that identified itself as closely connected to Edmonton (the closest urban center, approximately 45 miles away), welcomed light industry such as a waste facility. Conversely, residents from communities that identified with farming, fishing, and tourism activities viewed the facility as a threat to their way of life (Baxter and Greenlaw 2005).

Observations about siting hazardous waste facilities in the South provide important insights into community reactions. In Greensboro, NC, public trust and equity were significant factors and economic compensation was not, because the proposed incinerator offered few new jobs (Rabe 1994). Instead, the public desired "explicit guarantees against exploitation," including enhanced safety measures and assurances that the facility would serve only local and intrastate needs (Rabe 1994).

Attitudes regarding a proposed hazardous waste incinerator in Putnam County, WV, suggest a strong desire for protection of public health (Hunter and Leyden 1995). Phone interviews identified six distinct categories of concerns regarding the proposed incinerator. First among these concerns was health and safety (26 percent of the respondents). In general, respondents were concerned about whether the development process would run smoothly and whether the incinerator operations would be managed safely. Concerns about aesthetics and property values (2 percent) and lack of knowledge (2 percent) received less attention from respondents. As in the other studies, public trust was a recurring theme, particularly concerning public safety and the development and operation of the facility. An important difference between this study and others, however, is that participants in this situation were probably considering the choice of having the hazardous waste incinerator or not having it. This is not often the case for energy facilities because communities that need additional energy will build some sort of facility. Woody biomass should be compared to other fuels, not compared to the option of no facility.

EXPLORING PUBLIC PERCEPTIONS IN GAINESVILLE, FL

How the public perceives woody biomass may influence whether the developer proposes a wood-to-energy facility. Judging by seemingly low public knowledge about energy (National Environmental Education and Training Foundation 2002), well-designed education and outreach activities could have a significant impact on public attitudes. The development of such materials should be based on an understanding of what the public knows, does not know, and cares about with regard to woody biomass (Jacobson and others 2006). The literature on biomass from Europe and on hazardous waste facilities from North America provides insights to what the public might think about woody biomass, but it is difficult to know if these insights will hold true in the context of public perceptions of woody biomass developments in the South. Before effective outreach programs can be created, more research is needed into local knowledge and attitudes toward woody biomass in the South.

The Wood to Energy Outreach Program, developed in partnership between the University of Florida's School of Forest Resources and Conservation and the Forest Service, explored several strategies for understanding public perceptions about woody biomass. The project ran an intensive pilot program in Gainesville, FL, of developing materials and outreach procedures, including wood-to-energy community forums as models for community education.

Wood to Energy Outreach Program leaders conducted interviews with residents of two communities (Oconee County, SC, and Clay County, FL) with the aim of learning more about perceptions and concerns the public across the South. The project also conducted interviews with city commissioners in Gainesville, FL. Responses suggest that attitudes in the South are similar to those expressed in the literature, with respondents expressing concerns about the effects of forest management and harvesting on forest health and sustainability and the impacts on air quality from wood-burning facilities. Responses from the city commissioners indicated concern about the sustainability of local wood resources, increased truck traffic, increased entry-level job opportunities, and forestry forecasts in an area that is rapidly converting rural land to urban land uses. Most respondents said that they believed that woody biomass could be an economical energy source if environmental concerns were first addressed (Monroe and others 2009b).

In another research project, a sample was randomly selected from the tax roll of single family and mobile home owners in Alachua County, FL, where Gainesville is located. Mobile home owners were included in the sample to obtain a broad demographic profile. The mailed survey included questions on: (1) general awareness about woody biomass; (2) trust of sources of information; (3) attitudes about using wood for energy, sources of wood, and forest management; and (4) the respondents' demographics (Plate and others, in review). In general, survey results indicated that respondents (n = 302) were not very knowledgeable about using wood for energy and were confused about the relative advantages and disadvantages woody biomass when compared to fossil fuels, particularly about how the two energy sources affected global climate change. Respondents indicated that they were aware of their limited knowledge on the subject; nearly 50 percent responded to many knowledge questions by checking "I have no idea" and nearly 55 percent responded that they were "not at all knowledgeable" about the use of wood to generate electricity (Plate and others, in review).

While using waste wood from urban tree trimming and forestry activities appealed to a majority of those responding to this survey, the most important concern they reported regarding woody biomass was the protection and sustainability of nearby forests. For these respondents, solar and wind continued to represent more desirable sources of energy than woody biomass. Respondents indicated that they were more curious and interested than skeptical or fearful when informed that their region could support a woody biomass power facility. They also expressed a lack of confidence in local government (40 percent indicated low confidence) but revealed a markedly different attitude about the possibility of a local utility company managing a wood-fueled power plant (49 percent indicated fairly or highly confident). (In this particular community, the local utility is owned by the City of Gainesville.)

As shown in **table 7.1**, respondents to the survey identified local foresters, environmental groups, and extension agents as the most reliable sources of information about woody biomass, and representatives of private industry as the least reliable sources. Finally, 53 percent of the respondents expressed a belief that the community could be fairly or highly influential in a proposed project, and 54 percent said they were fairly or highly interested in participating in the decisionmaking process (Plate and others, in review).

PROVIDING INFORMATION AND ENGAGING THE PUBLIC

The Alachua County survey suggested that respondents are not very knowledgeable about woody biomass and were particularly confused about the carbon-neutral nature of wood as an energy source. Because initial public responses to the Gainesville City Commission's exploration of new sources of power drew criticism from citizens concerned about forest management and threats to forests under conservation protection, an outreach campaign on benefits of wood was not considered. People often do not respond well to persuasive messages that oppose their beliefs, and some people have been known to actively undermine policies they disagree with (Brehm and Brehm 1981).

Because half of the survey respondents suggested a willingness to be involved, we created a nonconfrontational process that encouraged engagement through questions and discussion. The

Table 7.1—Level of trust for various sources to provide reliable information about a wood-to-energy program

Source of information	Perceived reliability of information[a]
Local forester	2.2
Environmental group	2.2
Extension agent	2.1
Local utility company	1.9
Local newspaper	1.8
Private industry	1.6
Chamber of Commerce	1.6

[a] 1 = Not at all reliable; 3 = Very reliable.

objectives of this outreach activity were to provide information, enable experts and members of the community to interact and learn from each other, and collect feedback about participants' opinions, which could be shared with community decisionmakers (Monroe and others 2009a).

The Wood to Energy Community Forum was a 30-minute or 1-hour program, repeated several times at different locations over a 2-month period. It involved a 20- to 30-minute presentation by four or five experts who introduced their respective areas of expertise—forest management, the carbon cycle, technology, local supply of wood, and regional economic impact. Following the presentation, a forum facilitator encouraged the audience to ask questions of the experts. Participants completed a preforum and postforum survey about the forum. Attending 6 forums in November and December of 2006 were 172 community members from Gainesville, FL. Surveys were completed by 108 of these participants. Survey results suggested that participants learned from the forum and appreciated the opportunity to voice concerns and ask questions of experts. Their answers indicated that the participants would feel positive about a proposal to build a biomass energy facility, if the facility's design addressed their concerns (Monroe and others 2009a).

Our experience with the first community forum (a potentially hostile Sierra Club meeting) helped us revise our presentation, simplify our message, and focus more clearly on issues that lead to confusion. From our experience with the six forums, we offer the following advice to others who are planning community outreach activities:

- Simplify the information. Use graphics and photographs in the presentation, use analogies to explain concepts, and do not assume that people know much about energy, forest management, or economics. (Questions and comments from the audience helped us realize when we did and did not pitch the information to the appropriate level.)

- People want information but can be overwhelmed by too much information. Aim for enough information to generate reasonable questions and leave plenty of time for audience interaction. (Survey respondents marked the opportunity to ask questions as one of the important benefits of the forum.)
- Focus discussion on the comparison of reasonable options for meeting energy needs, rather than the impact of building a new facility compared to not building one, i.e., currently existing power plants. (A new facility will always generate more concerns and expenses than not having a new facility, but if additional energy is needed, then comparing reasonable strategies for obtaining that energy should be the focus.)
- Create an atmosphere that welcomes multiple perspectives and does not assume that the experts have the answer. The attitude of the experts as they present information is critical; asking participants to complete a survey helps them share information with the experts and organizers. (Survey respondents also rated the ability to access experts and the facilitator as important elements of a forum.)
- Work with existing community clubs and volunteer to hold a forum at one of their regularly scheduled meetings. This helps guarantee an audience and takes advantage of their publicity network, even though it may constrain the format or length of the forum. (Attendance at existing club meetings was much higher than at public forums we advertised.)

Strategies that enable organizers to compile feedback and convey citizen preferences to decisionmakers could be quite helpful in generating broad discussion and building trust. (We conducted pre- and postsurveys and shared the results with local city commissioners.)

Forums about energy sources in general can easily convey advantages and disadvantages about a number of different sources. A forum about only one source, e.g., wood, will risk the appearance of bias or advocacy. In such cases, it may be helpful to stress that there are many different strategies of using wood for energy and offer conflicting perspectives around these variations. (It was difficult to avoid promoting the use of wood for energy since that was the only topic of the forum. It would have been better to run a series of forums on energy, with wood being one of them.)

If people have little knowledge about woody biomass, it appears that they are satisfied with a "yes" or "no" answer to the simple question, "Should we use wood for energy?" As people learn more about the strategies for producing, hauling, and converting wood to energy, they are more likely to be interested in addressing the more insightful question, "What system best meets our needs for quality environment, community, and economy?" By taking time for broader issues associated with using wood for energy, people begin to consider related aspects, such as wood sources, harvesting, forest management, transportation, boiler technology,

scale, and fuel type. By supporting public discussion of criteria for an acceptable local woody biomass system, outreach strategies could give local decisionmakers the information they need about community perceptions and preferences.

SUMMARY

Public understanding and acceptance of woody biomass facilities is essential for the expansion of this energy source in the southern WUI. Although a significant number of sawmills, pulpmills, and small facilities have used wood for years to produce heat and power, the technology is relatively unknown among the general public. Surveys suggest that the public knows very little about energy in general, and even less about using wood for energy.

Developing educational and outreach materials that provide useful information requires an understanding of public perceptions and concerns. This literature review and the pilot program results suggest the following themes:

- While people look favorably on renewable energy sources in general, they view biomass energy production as comparatively less attractive than other renewable energy sources due to its relative similarity to fossil fuels. They do not understand carbon neutrality and are concerned about air pollution.
- Individuals within the immediate area of a proposed biomass power plant express concerns similar to those of people who live near other types of industrial facilities. These concerns include personal health and safety, environmental impacts, aesthetics of the landscape, increased noise, and increased traffic.
- The potential for mismanagement of forests that supply woody biomass is a very large public concern. To address the concern, it may be useful to develop guidelines that support sustainable forest operations as sources of woody biomass.
- Public trust in the developer and manager of the proposed bioenergy facility is a pivotal factor in how the public interprets the potential risks posed by a new facility.
- Also playing important roles in public perception are how a community perceives the relationship between rural sources of wood and urban demands for energy, and how community members identify their community's relationship to the WUI.
- Outreach opportunities that translate information into language that can be understood by the general public, and that offer interaction with subject experts could build trust, foster understanding, and help increase public acceptance of some types of wood-to-energy facilities.
- The public perceives forest agencies, extension agents, and environmental organizations as more trustworthy than industry and government.

In light of these observations, a successful outreach effort to educate local citizens and generate helpful discussion should explain why woody biomass is a renewable source of energy, distinguish woody biomass fuel from other energy sources, and address forest management and sustainability. For projects that aim to engage the public in developing an acceptable proposal, outreach efforts should also provide early and open communication between bioenergy facility developer(s) and the public, demonstrate how the proposal addresses questions and concerns voiced by the public, foster relationships with community leaders and partners who can help to build public trust in the proposed development, and jointly develop indicators to chart progress as the facility begins operation.

REFERENCES

Adams, M.D. 2003. Assessing awareness of Florida homeowners about the use of biomass for electricity production. Gainesville, FL: University of Florida. 74 p. M.S. thesis.

Bang, H.; Ellinger, A.E.; Hadjimarcou, J.; Traichal, P.A. 2000. Consumer concern, knowledge, belief, and attitude toward renewable energy: an application of the reasoned action theory. Psychology and Marketing. 17(6): 449–468.

Baxter, J.; Greenlaw, K. 2005. Explaining perceptions of a technological environmental hazard using comparative analysis. The Canadian Geographer. 49(1): 61–80.

Bliss, J.C.; Nepal, S.K.; Brooks, R.T.; Larsen, M.D. 1997. Forestry community or granfaloon? Journal of Forestry. 92: 6–10.

Bourke, L.; Luloff, A. 1994. Attitudes toward the management of nonindustrial private forest land. Society and Natural Resources. 7: 445–457.

Brehm, S.; Brehm, J.W. 1981. Psychological reactance: a theory of freedom and control. New York: Academic Press. 432 p.

Dickinson, J. 2005. Biomass energy, it can be renewable if done right. Suwannee-St. Johns Sierra Club Newsletter. March: 5–6.

Farhar, B. 1999. Willingness to pay for electricity from renewable resources: a review of utility market research. Golden, CO: U.S. Department of Energy, National Renewable Energy Laboratory: 9–14.

Greenpeace. 2007. Bioenergy. http://www.greenpeace.org/international/campaigns/climate-change/solutions/bioenergy. [Date accessed: February 7, 2007].

Hunter, S.; Leyden, K. 1995. Beyond NIMBY: explaining an opposition to hazardous waste facilities. Policy Studies Journal. 23(4): 601–619.

Ibiatayo, O. 2002. Public-private partnerships in the siting of hazardous waste facilities: the importance of trust. Waste Management & Research. 20: 212–222.

Ibitayo, O.; Pijawka, K. 1999. Reversing NIMBY: an assessment of State strategies for siting hazardous-waste facilities. Environment and Planning C: Government and Policy. 17: 379–389.

Jacobson, S.K.; McDuff, M.D.; Monroe, M.C. 2006. Conservation education and outreach techniques. Oxford, United Kingdom: Oxford University Press. 480 p.

Khan, J. 2004. Local politics of renewable energy: project planning, siting conflicts, and citizen participation. Lund, Sweden: Lund University. 93 p. Ph.D. dissertation.

Kunreuther, H.; Slovic, P.; MacGregor, D. 1996. Risk perception and trust: challenges for facility siting. Risk: Health, Safety & Environment. 7: 109–118.

Löfstedt, R. 1999. The role of trust in the North Blackforest: an evaluation of a citizen panel project. Risk: Health, Safety & Environment. 10: 7–30.

Monroe, M.C.; McDonell, L.; Oxarart, A.; Plate, R. 2009a. Using community forums to enhance public engagement in environmental issues. Journal of education for sustainable development. 3(2): 171-182.

Monroe, M.C.; Plate, R.; McDonell, L. 2009b. Wood to energy: technology transfer and education programs for Southern United States. In: Ashton, S.F.; Hubbard, W. G.; Rauscher, H. M., eds. A southern region conference on technology transfer and extension. Gen. Tech. Rep. SRS-116. Asheville, NC: U.S. Department of Agriculture, Forest Service, Southern Research Station: 74-83.

National Environmental Education and Training Foundation. 2002. Americans' low "energy IQ:" a risk to our energy future. Washington, DC: National Environmental Education and Training Foundation; RoperASW. 60 p.

National Renewable Energy Laboratory. 2009. Learning about renewable energy. Biomass energy basics. http://www.nrel.gov/learning/re_biomass.html. [Date accessed: January 13, 2010].

Natural Resources Defense Council. 2003. Biomass energy. Clean air & energy: energy. http://www.nrdc.org/air/energy/fbiom.asp. [Date accessed: February 7, 2007].

Plate, R.; Monroe, M.C.; Oxarart, A. [In review]. Public perceptions of using woody biomass as a renewable energy source. Journal of Extension.

Rabe, B. 1994. Beyond NIMBY: hazardous waste citing in Canada and the United States. Washington, DC: Brookings Institution Press: 106–109.

Rohracher, H.; Bogner, T.; Späth, P.; Faber, F. 2004. Improving the public perception of bioenergy in the EU. European Commission - Directorate-General for Energy and Transport, Brussels. http://ec.europa.eu/energy/res/sectors/doc/bioenergy/bioenergy_perception.pdf. [Date accessed: April 8, 2007].

Rosch, C.; Kaltschmitt, M. 1999. Energy from biomass—do non-technical barriers prevent an increase use? Biomass and Bioenergy. 16: 347–356.

Shields, D.J.; Martin, I.M.; Martin, W.E.; Haefele, M.A. 2002. Survey results of the American public's values, objectives, beliefs, and attitudes regarding forests and grasslands: a technical document supporting the 2000 USDA Forest Service RPA Assessment. Gen. Tech. Rep. RMRS-GTR-95. Fort Collins, CO: U.S. Department of Agriculture Forest Service, Rocky Mountain Research Station. 111 p. http://www.fs.fed.us/rm/pubs/rmrs_gtr095.pdf. [Date accessed: February 7, 2007].

Sierra Club. 2007. Sierra Club conservation policies: biomass guidance. http://www.sierraclub.org/policy/conservation/biomass.asp. [Date accessed: January 17, 2007].

Sinclair, K.; Knuth, B.A. 2000. Non-industrial private forest landowner use of geographic data: a precondition for ecosystem-based management. Society and Natural Resources. 13(6): 521–536.

Sinclair, P.; Löfstedt, R. 2001. The influence of trust in a biomass plant application: the case study of Sutton, UK. Biomass and Bioenergy. 21: 177–184.

Tarrant, M.A.; Porter, R.; Cordell, H.K. 2002. Sociodemographics, values, and attitudes. In: Wear, D.N.; Greis, J.G., eds. Southern forest resource assessment. Gen. Tech. Rep. SRS–53. Asheville, NC: U.S. Department of Agriculture Forest Service, Southern Research Station: 175–187. Chapter 7.

Toivonen, R.; Ramo, A-K.; Tahvanainen, L. 2002. Perspectives on the supply of bio-mass from private forests in Finland. In: 12th European conference on biomass for energy, industry and climate protection. Florence, IT: ETA Renewable Energies: 87–90.

Upreti, B.R. 2004. Conflict over biomass energy development in the United Kingdom: some observations and lessons from England and Wales. Energy Policy. 32: 785–800.

U.S. Department of Agriculture Forest Service. 2004. Southern forest resource assessment. http://www.srs.fs.usda.gov/sustain/. [Date accessed: February 25, 2008].

U.S. Department of Commerce, U.S. Census Bureau. 2005. Nevada edges out Arizona as the fastest-growing State. Public Information Office, U.S. Census Bureau Press Release. December 22, 2005. CB05–187. http://www.census.gov/Press-Release/www/releases/archives/population/006142.html. [Date accessed: February 25, 2008].

U.S. Department of Commerce, U.S. Census Bureau. 2008. National and State population estimates, cumulative estimates of population change for the United States. Reg8 (NST–EST2008–02). http://www.census.gov/popest/states/NST-pop-chg.html. [Date accessed: June 16, 2009].

van den Hoogen, W.M.; Hubner, G.; Meijinders, A.L.; Midden, C J.H. 2002. Biomass: how people think and feel about it. In: 12th European conference on biomass for energy, industry and climate protection. Florence IT: ETA Renewable Energies: 1086-1089.

van der Horst, D. 2005. UK biomass energy since 1990: the mismatch between project types and policy objectives. Energy Policy. 33: 705–716.

van der Horst, D.; Sinclair, P.; Löfstedt, R. 2002. Public participation in decision support for regional biomass energy planning. Serie A. Options Mediterraneennes. 48: 123–130.

EDITORS AND AUTHORS

Compiling Editors

Christie Staudhammer	Assistant professor (Forest Biometrics)	University of Florida School of Forest Resources and Conservation	349 Newins-Ziegler Hall P.O. Box 110410 Gainesville, FL 32611-0410	352-846-3503 staudham@ufl.edu
L. Annie Hermansen-Báez	Center manager/ technology transfer coordinator	U.S. Department of Agriculture Forest Service Southern Research Station InterfaceSouth	Building 164, Mowry Road P.O. Box 110806 Gainesville, FL 32611	352-376-3271 ahermansen@fs.fed.us
Douglas R. Carter	Professor (Forest Economics and Management)	University of Florida School of Forest Resources and Conservation	357 Newins-Ziegler Hall P.O. Box 110410 Gainesville, FL 32611-0410	352-846-0893 drcart@ufl.edu
Edward A. Macie	Regional urban forester	Forest Service U.S. Department of Agriculture Region 8	1720 Peachtree Road Atlanta, GA 30309	404-347-1647 emacie@fs.fed.us

Authors

Chapter 1

| Christie Staudhammer | Assistant professor (Forest Biometrics) | University of Florida School of Forest Resources and Conservation | 349 Newins-Ziegler Hall P.O. Box 110410 Gainesville, FL 32611-0410 | 352-846-3503 staudham@ufl.edu |

Chapter 2

Christie Staudhammer (lead author)	Assistant professor (Forest Biometrics)	University of Florida School of Forest Resources and Conservation	349 Newins-Ziegler Hall P.O. Box 110410 Gainesville, FL 32611-0410	352-846-3503 staudham@ufl.edu
Richard Schroeder	President and founder	BioResource Management, Inc.	3520 NW 43rd Street Gainesville, FL 32606	352-377-8282 rs@bio-resource.com
Brian Becker	Ph.D. student	University of Florida School of Natural Resources and Environment	P.O. Box 110831 Gainesville, FL 32611-0831	brbecker@ufl.edu
Matthew H. Langholtz	Biomass consultant	Oak Ridge National Laboratory	PO Box 2008 MS6422 Oak Ridge, TN 37831-6422	865-574-6520 langholtzmh@ornl.gov

Chapter 3

Richard Schroeder	President and founder	BioResource Management, Inc.	3520 NW 43rd Street Gainesville, FL 32606	352-377-8282 rs@bio-resource.com

Chapter 4

Phil Badger (lead author)	Technical director	U.S. Department of Energy SSEB Biomass State and Regional Partnership	3115 Northington Court P.O. Box 26 Florence, AL 35630	256-740-5634 pbadger@ bioenergyupdate.com
Pratap Pullammanappallil	Assistant Professor	University of Florida Agricultural and Biological Engineering	P.O. Box 110570 Gainesville, FL US 32611-0570	352-392-1864

Chapter 5

Matthew H. Langholtz (lead author)	Biomass consultant	Oak Ridge National Laboratory	PO Box 2008 MS6422 Oak Ridge, TN 37831-6422	865-574-6520 langholtzmh@ornl.gov
Douglas R. Carter	Professor (Forest Economics and Management)	University of Florida School of Forest Resources and Conservation	357 Newins-Ziegler Hall P.O. Box 110410 Gainesville, FL 32611-0410	352-846-0893 drcart@ufl.edu
Richard Schroeder	President and founder	BioResource Management, Inc.	3520 NW 43rd Street Gainesville, FL 32606	352-377-8282 rs@bio-resource.com

Chapter 6

Alan W. Hodges	Extension scientist	University of Florida Food and Economic Resources Department	1115 MCCB P.O. Box 110240 IFAS Gainesville, FL 32611-0240	352-392-1881 Ext. 312 awhodges@ufl.edu

Chapter 7

Martha C. Monroe (lead author)	Professor	University of Florida School of Forest Resources and Conservation	347 Newins-Zeigler Hall P.O. Box 110410 Gainesville, FL 32611	352-846-0878 mcmonroe@ufl.edu
Richard Plate	Graduate Student	University of Florida School of Natural Resources and Environment	P.O. Box 116455 Gainesville, FL 32611	richarp@ufl.edu
Lauren McDonell	Former wood to energy coordinator	University of Florida School of Forest Resources and Conservation	Newins-Zeigler Hall P.O. Box 110410 Gainesville, FL 32611	970-884-3182 mcdonell@ufl.edu
Annie Oxarart	Wood to energy coordinator	University of Florida School of Forest Resources and Conservation	Newins-Zeigler Hall P.O. Box 110410 Gainesville, FL 32611	352-846-0144 oxarart@ufl.edu

www.ingramcontent.com/pod-product-compliance
Lightning Source LLC
Chambersburg PA
CBHW081226280526
45787CB00006B/2547